DAD'S ARMY
The Lost Episodes

DAD'S ARMY
The Lost Episodes

Jimmy Perry
&
David Croft

Virgin

First published in 1998 by
Virgin Publishing Limited
Thames Wharf Studios
Rainville Road
London W6 9HT

Copyright © Jimmy Perry & David Croft 1998

Thanks to Hulton Getty and the BBC for permission to use the photographs
in this book, and special thanks to Don Smith for finding the photographs
from the second series.

A catalogue record for this book is available from the British Library.

ISBN 1 85227 757 2

Designed by Design 23, London
Repro by Colourwise Ltd, Sussex
Printed and bound in Great Britain by Hilman Printers (Frome) Ltd.

Contents

Introduction by
David Croft **6**

Introduction by
Jimmy Perry **8**

Episode 7
Operation Kilt **11**

Episode 8
The Battle of Godfrey's Cottage . . . **35**

Episode 9
**The Loneliness of the
Long Distance Walker** **59**

Episode 10
Sgt. Wilson's Little Secret **85**

Episode 11
A Stripe for Frazer **109**

Episode 12
Under Fire **135**

Introduction by
David Croft

I suppose I should count myself very lucky. Out of more than 400 programmes that I have produced and, with Jimmy Perry, Jeremy Lloyd and Richard Spendlove, co-written, all are safely stored in the BBC archives on the shelves ready for viewing - bar the six that are featured in this book.

The tapes of these scripts and of many others such as *Steptoe & Son*, *Till Death Us Do Part* and of the early black and white shows such as *Hugh and I* were wiped for two very good reasons. First, the two inch tape that they were recorded on was a new and very expensive invention. I seem to remember that each one cost £600 which was a large sum to come out of the show budget at that time. It was, in fact, a star performer's salary. For this reason, a special department was set up at the BBC to service used tapes, repair them and return them to the programme departments to be used a second or even a third time. A 'used' tape represented a much lower figure against the cost of a programme and we were always struggling against shortage of money. Secondly, Equity, the actors' trade union, went to great lengths to keep actors in employment by working on new shows, rather than allowing air time to be over crowded with repeats. To this end, they refused to allow shows to be repeated more than two years after the first transmission. Thus, when two years had expired there was no agreement to permit any further showing of a programme.

One of the factors which helped to save my programmes from destruction was that I was on the staff and, therefore, always present when a piece of paper came round requiring a producer's agreement for a show to be wiped. I always contrived to withold consent. I can only conclude that when the necessary form appeared for these six programmes I must have been on holiday.

Dad's was sold overseas and was particularly popular in New Zealand and Australia. In order to achieve these sales, the programmes were recorded on 16mm film by the simple process of sticking a camera in front of a very bright television tube and shooting away with rather grainy results. Over the years I have sent letters and telegrammmes to New Zealand and Australia and in fact paid personal visits to search for copies but none have shown up. Jimmy and I came to the conclusion that

This photo was taken in 1969 during the filming of one of the last black and white episodes.

the likelihood of finding them now is really pretty remote, so we decided to publish the scripts.

The Battle of Godfrey's Cottage was always a particular favourite of mine. The idea of Godfrey and his sisters putting lace doilies on their polished tables to save them from being scratched by a gun had a special appeal to my sense of humour. These scripts also fill in some of the important details regarding Sergeant Wilson's relationship with Mrs Pike and with the boy Pike, and the mystery surrounding Private Walker's call up.

All these scripts bring back happy memories to Jimmy and me. We little realised when we were writing these shows the enormous affection the public were to have for them. I was particularly touched a few weeks ago when a journalist in a national paper, discussing *Dad's Army* and BBC comedy, paraphrased Churchill and wrote 'This was their finest half hour.'

David Croft

Introduction by
Jimmy Perry

Earlier this year I was sitting in a taxi with Clive Dunn. We had not seen each other for quite some time but he had hardly changed and as we rattled on about 'the old days' he said, 'I can't believe I did it. It was all magic, like a fairytale.' It certainly was a fairytale. Everything was right about it, the subject, the time, the cast and the script, but without David Croft's persistence I very much doubt if *Dad's Army* would ever have seen the light of day. Ours had been a strange partnership. At first, apart from the fact that we both knew what was funny, it seemed that we had very little in common but as time went by we realised we had quite a lot. Both singers (David a tenor and I a baritone), both served in the Royal Artillery during the war (David a major and I a sergeant), both had been to public schools (David to Rugby and I to St Paul's) and both had to leave early (David because the money ran out and I because I was tired of being thrashed). Both wine buffs and both had the same motto 'never take no for an answer'. We would probably never have met in the first place but for the fact that Ann, David's wife, was my agent at the time. No doubt she put pressure on him to give me some work as an actor and it was in the BBC TV comedy series *Hugh and I*, which David produced, that we first met. Perhaps he had an off day or perhaps it was my performance, but I thought, 'he looks a bit grim, I'd better mind my Ps and Qs.' Ann Croft was an excellent agent and over the next two or three years she dragged poor David to see me in various theatre shows. By now I had thought up the idea for *Dad's Army* and I had written a first script which I called *The Fighting Tigers*. I just didn't know who to show it to and had put it in the drawer of my desk where it remained for some time. One day Ann phoned and said David was doing a comedy series called *Beggar My Neighbour* and there was a small part in it for me. It was during the rehearsals for that show that I gave David my script to read, and the rest is history. So, but for those forces of destiny, *The Fighting Tigers* would have ended up in the drawer of my desk or in a wastepaper basket at the BBC.

Since *Dad's Army* started thirty years ago, many people have leapt into print with books about the Home Guard. Most of them were not even born when it was in existence. Well, I may have been just a very immature teenager, but I remember because I was there!

Was the Home Guard a worthwhile undertaking? Most certainly. It gave ordinary citizens, at least ordinary male citizens, a feeling that they were engaged in a great enterprise and it was an important morale-builder. As time went by, the Home Guard became a well-armed auxiliary force and released large numbers of the regular army for active service.

The Home Guard was a British organisation; improvisation and eccentricity at its very best. I can remember our commanding officer in the Watford Home Guard having a special revolver holster designed so that it strapped to his thigh. This gave him a quick 'draw', which he demonstrated to us at the end of each parade. He would then wave his revolver in the air and shout 'Kill Germans!' We would wave our rifles and shout back 'Kill, kill, kill!' and then dismiss.

Our enthusiasm verged on the fanatical. He decided to form all of us teenage boys into a commando unit and designed a special badge with a large 'C' which we wore on our shoulders. We loved it and revelled in the special weapons we were issued with: a wire cheese cutter for creeping up behing Nazi sentries and decapiataing them; sharpened bicycle chains for close combat; razor-sharp knives and knuckle dusters. These were topped off with P17 rifles, which we carried everywhere. However, we were not allowed to take any ammunition home; this was only to be issued in case of an invasion.

The sight of us young boys swaggering down the street, armed to the teeth, would have sent a modern-day social worker screaming into the bushes. Our training never stopped and quite often took the form of competitions. A favourite was rather like the *Generation Game*. It involved two Lewis guns and two blindfolded contestants who would strip down the machine guns and reassemble them. They were encouraged by cheers from the rest of the platoon and our potty CO with a stopwatch shouting, 'Hurry up, the Nazis are coming!' There was also the wonderful comradeship: booze-ups, dances, and of course, our concert party – every unit had one. Make no mistake, it was our finest hour. We stood alone against the most evil tyranny the world had ever seen. To be alive at that time was to experience the British people at their best and at perhaps the greatest moment in their history. I remember one beautiful summer evening in 1940 while on duty with an old World War One veteran and saying, 'What do I do if the Germans come, Corporal?' He looked at me and replied, 'If the Germans come, son, you'll do as you're bloody well told.' But they never did come.

Jimmy Perry

Jimmy and David pose with one of the BBC's new colour cameras in 1969.

DAD'S ARMY NO. 7

Operation Kilt

CAST

Capt. George Mainwaring ....Arthur Lowe

Sgt. Arthur Wilson ....John Le Mesurier

L/Cpl. Jack Jones ....Clive Dunn

Pte. James Frazer ....John Laurie

Pte. Joe Walker ....James Beck

Pte. Charles Godfrey...............................Arnold Ridley

Pte. Frank Pike ....Ian Lavender

Mrs Pike..Janet Davies

Capt. Ogilvy..James Copeland

Pte. Sponge ....Colin Bean

Remainder of Platoon...........................Richard Jacques
Frank Godfrey
Alec Coleman
Hugh Cecil
Jimmy Mac
Desmond Callum-Jones
Vic Taylor
David Seaforth
Richard Kitteridge

Shooting The Pantomime Cow

In this script, we wrote long sequences in the yard of the church hall, and for two reasons decided to play these in the studio. First, our budget was pretty tight, and going down to Honington School yard to shoot the scenes on film, with all the attendant expense of the entire cast and crew, was simply not to be afforded. Secondly, our whole operation was based on the actors playing to the audience in the studio and timing and reacting to their laughter. This was always an uppermost requirement in our minds because nothing can replace good actors playing to a live audience. I think it is sometimes the failure to pay attention to this principle that affects programmes produced today.

We therefore decided not to write any scenes in the church hall, with the result that we had only Mainwaring's bank office in one corner of the studio, leaving the rest of the studio space for the yard. Later in the recording, Paul Joel, the designer, reset the yard with vegetation and trees for a scene in the woods. We could get away with this visually because the action took place at night, and the studio light could be arranged so that we didn't see anything we didn't want to see.

All that remained to be shot on film was the scene where the pantomime cow got mixed up with a herd of real cows. Nobody knew how the animals were going to behave when this happened; after all, whoever in their right minds would put a panto cow into a field with real cows? The result was hilarious. The cows were completely bewildered and so too was our Scottish cameraman, Jimmy Balfour, who tried to put slates with scene and shot numbers before the shot of each cow.

'Forget all that rubbish!' I yelled. 'Keep turning over – we'll sort it out later.' This was pure heresy to any BBC cameraman, but Jimmy Balfour did it and, as a result, we got one of the funniest scenes we ever shot.

When it came to the last scene, we were a bit concerned at the prospect of stringing Clive Dunn and James Copeland (who played Captain Ogilvie) upside down by the ankles. We therefore called for two volunteers from our trusty platoon to double for the actors. The ever-reliable Colin Bean volunteered to double for Ogilvie and Richard Jaques for Clive Dunn. On the recording we performed a bit of a conjuring trick by hiding the pair of them behind straw and heaving them aloft by the ankles – well padded – on cue. Having achieved this, they could then be lowered behind the straw and magically Clive and James could re-emerge. It worked like a dream!

David Croft

SCENES

1.	**SIDE OFFICE CHURCH HALL**
2.	**YARD OUTSIDE CHURCH HALL**
3.	**YARD OUTSIDE THE CHURCH HALL THE NEXT EVE**
4.	**YARD A LITTLE LATER**
5.–10.	**TELECINE**
11.	**YARD THE NEXT EVENING**
12.	**YARD LATER**
13.	**TELECINE**
14.	**WOODS – NIGHT**
15.	**WOODS – NIGHT**

SCENE 1.
SIDE OFFICE CHURCH HALL.

MAINWARING IS SITTING AT HIS DESK, HE IS READING A NEWSPAPER.
WILSON ENTERS.

WILSON   Ah, there you are, sir, you left the bank early, didn't you?

MAIN   Yes, I had a lot of paperwork to get on with.

WILSON   I see.

MAIN   (RUSTLING THE NEWSPAPER) I've finished it now.

WILSON   I was just wondering why you left the bank by the back door.

MAIN   There's no reason why I can't leave by the back door, is there, Wilson?

WILSON   None whatsoever, sir, but I did just happen to notice that as you were leaving by the back door Mr Green from Head Office was coming through the front door.

MAIN   Really, what did he want?

WILSON   Well he seemed a bit cross, sir, he said this is the third time this week he's missed you. And he took a rather dim view of all those war posters in the bank.

MAIN   Doesn't he know there's a war on?

WILSON   Yes, sir, but he feels they rather clash with ours.

MAIN   Oh, why is that?

WILSON   Well, underneath one of our posters which says 'Let us invest your money', you've put one that says 'Trust no one, careless talk costs lives.'

MAIN   Just an unfortunate coincidence.

WILSON   I'm sure it was, sir. But you also put 'Don't be a squander bug like me', underneath the portrait of the founder of the bank.

MAIN   Oh, I can't be bothered with all that rubbish, listen to this. (READS) Tribesmen on the N.W. Frontier of India and the staff of the Khyber Agency have contributed £1,200 to the Spitfire Fund, hum, what's our Spitfire Fund stand at now?

WILSON	£4/7/6d, sir.
MAIN	I don't see why a lot of savage tribesman should do better than our lads.

> At this time, of course, the British Raj ruled over the entire continent of India from the southernmost tip of Ceylon (Sri Lanka) to the Khyber Pass in the far north.

WILSON	They probably held some local merchant to ransom. Our lads can hardly go and kidnap the manager of Sainsbury's.
MAIN	Yes – it's pretty tough out there. I had an uncle who commanded a unit there – Fruity Mainwaring – finished up a nervous wreck. You've got to be ready for anything. I mean, you might be sitting in a room, when all of a sudden there would be a blood curdling scream and through the door would come a wild-eyed hairy tribesman armed to the teeth.

(THERE IS A YELL FROM OUTSIDE THE DOOR AND THE SOUND OF DUSTLIDS. THE DOOR FLIES OPEN AND CPL. JONES STAGGERS IN WITH HIS HAT OVER HIS EYES, GRASPING HIS RIFLE. WILSON DIVES UNDER THE DESK)

JONES	(OUT OF BREATH) Permission to speak, sir? I'm sorry, Mr Mainwaring, it's that booby trap outside the door. I forgot all about it. (HE STARES AT WILSON WHO IS GETTING UP) What's the matter with Mr Wilson, sir?
MAIN	He thought he was on the N.W. Frontier, Cpl.
JONES	Really, sir, I had a brother who serves on the N.W. Frontier in the Khyber Pass – in fact, that's where he got wounded. Them's the boys them Pathoms, just like the Fuzzie Wuzzies: they come at you with the cold, cold steel, and chop right up.

> This would have been the equivalent to 2p in modern currency, which today would buy half an Oxo cube.

MAIN	What is it you want, Cpl.?
JONES	Well, I thought I'd be the first one to bring you the good news. The meat ration's gone up 1/10d to 2/2d.
MAIN	Thank you, Cpl. Jones, that's a great comfort.
JONES	But I'm afraid butter's gone down two ounces. But the fat ration's still at eight ounces, so that means you can have six of marge and two of butter, or four of marge, two of cooking fat and two of butter, or four of cooking fat, two of marge and two of butter or three of cooking fat, three of marge and two of butter, or four of marge and four of cooking fat or eight of marge.
WILSON	Yes, thank you, Jones, you've been a great help. Oh, by the way, sir, this packet came for you at the bank just after you left. (HE HANDS MAIN A LARGE ENVELOPE)
JONES	(TO WILSON) Of course, if you felt like it, you could have six of cooking fat and two of butter … (HE RAMBLES ON)
MAIN	(READING) That's the ticket, that will soon get rid of some excess fat.
JONES	You can't have any excess fat, sir. I've told you, you can either have two of …
MAIN	(SHOUTING) Jones! Listen to this, Wilson. In future all H.G. Units will do 15

minutes P.T. before parade. Right, we'll start tonight.

WILSON   Tonight, sir. But who's going to take us?

MAIN   I am, of course, here's all the instructions. (HE HOLDS UP HANDBOOK) All right, Jones, parade the men outside in the yard, there's nothing like plenty of fresh air when you're doing P.T. And, Jones, tell them to strip off.

JONES   Strip off. Yes, sir. (HE SALUTES AND GOES)

WILSON   Wait a minute, sir, Capt. Ogilvie of the Highland Regiment is due here at 19.30 to brief us about the night manoeuvres on Saturday.

MAIN   19.30? (LOOKS AT HIS WATCH) That'll be in about ...

WILSON   7.30, sir.

MAIN   I know, Wilson. Well, it's only 6.30 now, we've got plenty of time.

WILSON   But don't you think you're being a bit hasty, sir. After all you don't know anything about P.T.

MAIN   (COLDLY) When we took arms in the hour of our country's need, we didn't know anything about a lot of things, Sergeant. But I've never let you down yet, have I?

WILSON   Well, er ...

MAIN   That will be all, Sergeant. Outside and strip off.

FADE.

SCENE 2
YARD OUTSIDE THE CHURCH HALL.

THE MEN ARE DRAWN UP ON PARADE. L/CPL. JONES IS STANDING IN FRONT.

JONES   Now look here – I'm giving you an order. Capt. Mainwaring says you've got to strip off.

FRAZER   Strip off for what?

JONES   The Captain's going to give us some P.T.

FRAZER   (INDICATING GODFREY) He can't strip off. It's only his clothes keeping him from falling apart.

In this scene from the very first episode of *Dad's Army*, the platoon have not yet been issued with uniforms or proper weapons. Jonesy is wearing his Old Contemptibles' uniform from the 1914-18 war.

WALKER	Well, I'm not stripping off in this draughty yard. Besides, people can see us from the road.
JONES	Look, I don't want any insubordination.

(MAIN AND WILSON ENTER)

	Squad, attention. (HE SALUTES)
JONES	Well, sir. They er ... (HE QUICKLY STARTS TO STRIP OFF) Well, I'm ready, sir.
MAIN	Thank you, Jones. All right, stand them at ease, Sergeant.
WILSON	Platoon, stand at ease. Easy!
MAIN	Right, now pay attention, men. I've just had an order from G.H.Q. that we are to do 15 minutes P.T. before every parade. If we're going to beat the Hun, we must be fit in every way, with clean bodies and clean minds. Now, I've never asked you to do anything that I wouldn't do myself, so, on the command strip, we shall all strip together.

(JONES IS SHIVERING)

JONES	(WITH HIS TEETH CHATTERING) Per... per... per... mission to speak, sir.

MAIN   What is it, Jones?

JONES   It ain't half chilly out here. Can't we go inside.

MAIN   Certainly not, if you're cold, start running on the spot.

JONES   Yes, sir. (HE STARTS RUNNING)

MAIN   All right, men, strip.

(THEY ALL START TO STRIP TO THE WAIST EXCEPT WILSON. FRAZER HAS SEVERAL TATTOOS ON HIS ARM)

WALKER   (POINTING TO TATTOOS) I can see your naval, 'taf'.

(HE LAUGHS)

FRAZER   It's nothing to laugh at, these cost me quite a few bob.

WALKER   'Ere, what's this one, 'A boy's friend is his "mot"'. What's a 'mot'?

FRAZER   Mother, you stupid sassanack. I couldn't afford the HER.

GODFREY   (TO MAIN) Excuse me, sir?

MAIN   What is it, Godfrey?

GODFREY   Do you want me to remove my binder.

MAIN   Your what?

GODFREY   My flannel binder. Shall I take it off?

MAIN   Of course.

GODFREY   Well would you mind holding the safety pin for a minute. (HE STARTS TO UNWIND)

MAIN   Oh – keep it on – we shall be here all day.

KID'S VOICE   Look at that hairy chest.

MAIN   Who said that, Wilson?

WILSON   It's some boys playing in the churchyard.

MAIN   Well tell them to go away at once.

WILSON   Go away at once, you boys.

VOICE   Why aren't you taking your clothes off as well, big bonse.

MAIN   (TO WILSON) Yes, why aren't you taking ... I mean (SHOUTS) clear off at once, you boys wouldn't be laughing at us like that if the Germans came.

VOICE   No. But the Germans would.

MAIN   If you don't go away at once I shall clear the churchyard.

VOICE   All right, baldy, keep your shirt on.

(THEY RUN OFF LAUGHING)

MAIN   We'll have a word with Miss Beckwith and have that ginger-haired one kept in after school.

> Most elderly gentlemen in Victorian and Edwardian times wore a flannel binder over their underwear. This was in the days before central heating, of course.

(MRS PIKE ENTERS)

MAIN   Now then – on the command 'Spring' – I want you all to -

MRS PIKE   (TO MAIN) I'm sorry to interrupt like this, Mr Mainwaring, but you see …
(SHE BREAKS OFF) Why have you all got your clothes off?

WILSON   Oh, Mavis, please, can't you see we're busy?

MAIN   Well, Mrs Pike, what is it? We're just about to start some P.T.

MRS PIKE   Oh, I see, well don't let Frank stand around too long like that will you, Mr Mainwaring.
I don't want him to start with his chest again.

MAIN   Don't worry, Mrs Pike. He'll soon warm up.

MRS PIKE   Why have you still got your shirt on, Arthur?

MAIN   Yes, hurry up, Wilson.

WILSON   I don't think it would be very good for discipline, sir.

MAIN   What are you talking about?

WILSON   (DROPPING HIS VOICE) Well, you see, sir. I'm afraid I've got a rather large hole in
my vest.

MRS PIKE   You didn't put that vest on again this morning, did you, Arthur? I told you to leave it
out for me to mend.

WILSON   Please, Mavis, not so loud.

MRS PIKE   (IN A LOUD WHISPER) Well take your shirt and vest off together, then no one will
notice. You've got nothing to be ashamed of with your body, Arthur, you know.
Mr Mainwaring, he's got a lovely physique when he strips off.

WILSON   (PURPLE) Mavis, please.

(WILSON QUICKLY STRIPS OFF AND STANDS LOOKING VERY SHEEPISH)

MRS PIKE   That's better. He does look nice, doesn't he, Mr Mainwaring?

MAIN   What is it you want, Mrs Pike?

MRS PIKE   Oh yes, I nearly forgot. (SHE TAKES A RIFLE BOLT OUT OF HER HANDBAG) I
think this is part of Frank's gun, he left it behind. Is it important?

MAIN   (TAKING IT) Yes, Mrs Pike, it is very important. (HE CROSSES TO FRANK PIKE)
What's this, Pike?

PIKE   It's a rifle bolt, sir.

MAIN   I know what it is, you stupid boy. It belongs to your rifle.

PIKE   I'm sorry, sir, I must have forgotten to put it back when I cleaned it.

MRS PIKE   You left it on the draining board, Frank. I'm afraid I washed it up with the tea things.
Anyhow, there's no harm done. I must be off now, don't let him stand around too long
without his jacket on will you, Mr Mainwaring.   (SHE GOES)

MAIN   (HANDING THE BOLT TO FRANK) I'll talk to you later, Pike. Now hold on to this
and don't loose it.

(PIKE IS WEARING A THICK WOOLLEN VEST AND HE SLIPS THE BOLT DOWN THE
FRONT OF IT)

(JONES IS STILL RUNNING ON THE SPOT)

    MAIN   That'll do, Jones.

(JONES STOPS)

        Warmer now?

    JONES   Yes, sir. Dizzy, but warmer.

    MAIN   See he doesn't keel over, Walker. Now, perhaps we can start. Give me the manual, Sergeant.

(WILSON HANDS IT TO HIM)

        Here we are, deep breathing. Stand with your legs apart, hands on hips and chest out and breathe in through the nose and out through the mouth. Well that's fairly simple. Have you got that?

(THEY ARE ALL STANDING IN THE CORRECT POSITION WITH BOTH HANDS ON THEIR HIPS, EXCEPT GODFREY, WHO ONLY HAS ONE ON HIS HIP)

        It's both hands on the hips, Godfrey.

    GODFREY   Oh I'm so sorry, sir.

    MAIN   Right, men, are you ready? Now then, stand to attention. Jumping aside with the feet and arms at the same time like this. (HE SHOWS THEM)

    WILSON   Shall I hold the manual, sir?

    MAIN   Excellent idea, Sgt.

(WILSON TAKES THE MANUAL AND HOLDS IT FOR MAIN TO READ WHILE HE IS DOING THE EXERCISE)

        Are you ready, go!

(THEY ALL START THE EXERCISE EXCEPT WILSON WHO IS HOLDING THE BOOK)

        Don't joggle the book up and down like that, Wilson, I can't read the instructions.

    WILSON   If you don't mind me saying so, sir, it's not the book that's joggling up and down, it's you.

    MAIN   Platoon halt. Now I ... I ... (HE IS GASPING FOR BREATH) I bet you feel better for that, don't you, men. What's next?

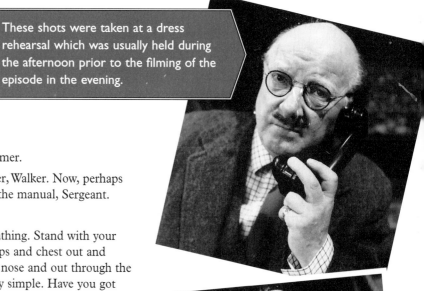

These shots were taken at a dress rehearsal which was usually held during the afternoon prior to the filming of the episode in the evening.

No one noticed that Mainwaring's moustache was fixed upside down during the rehearsal, although it was the right way up again for filming.

WILSON   Press ups, sir.

MAIN   Ah yes. (WILSON IS STILL HOLDING THE BOOK FOR MAIN TO READ) Everyone face down on the floor. (MAIN GETS DOWN ON THE FLOOR, WILSON KNEELS DOWN BESIDE HIM STILL HOLDING THE BOOK) Now then, on the command one, you will slowly raise yourselves up, hold it and then lower yourselves to the floor. Right now! (MAIN TRIES TO RAISE HIMSELF AND FALLS)

WILSON   Allow me, sir. (HE GRIPS MAIN BY THE BACK OF HIS TROUSERS AND PULLS)

MAIN   Thank you, Wilson, two. (WITH WILSON'S HELP HE LOWERS HIMSELF AGAIN, HE DOES THIS SEVERAL TIMES, ONLY A FEW OF THE REST OF THE PLATOON CAN RAISE THEMSELVES . . . THE REST LIE FACE DOWN)

MAIN   Right, on the feet, up. (WILSON HELPS MAIN TO HIS FEET. THE REST OF THE PLATOON STRUGGLE UP)

WILSON   Circumrotary trunk movements next, sir.

MAIN   (WHO IS ALL IN) All right Wilson, let me get my breath back. (THE WHOLE PLATOON IS NOW ON ITS FEET WITH THE EXCEPTION OF JONES WHO IS STILL LYING FLAT ON HIS FACE) What's the matter with Jones? (HE CROSSES TO HIM) Get up, Jones. (HE KNEELS DOWN AND SHOUTS IN HIS EAR) Jones!

JONES   (RAISING HIMSELF ON HIS ELBOW) Oh I'm sorry, sir, I must have just dozed off. (HE GETS UP)

MAIN   Not bad, men, not bad at all.

WILSON   Circumrotary trunk movements next, sir.

MAIN   (ICY) I shall decide what's next, Wilson, and now, men, I think we'll finish up with a simple exercise, touching our toes a half a dozen times. Right begin. (MAIN RAISES HIS ARMS ABOVE HIS HEAD AND SWINGS DOWN TO TOUCH HIS TOES, HE GIVES A HOWL OF AGONY, HE IS STUCK)

WILSON   Are you all right, sir?

MAIN   It's my lumbago, well don't just stand there, do something.

WILSON   (TO JONES) Quick, get a chair.

(JONES RUSHES INTO THE HALL. THE REST OF THE PLATOON BREAK RANKS AND CROWD ROUND)

WALKER   Shall I get the doctor, Sgt.?

FRAZER   You'd be better off getting a new P.T. instructor.

(JONES COMES OUT WITH A CHAIR)

JONES   Here you are, Mr Mainwaring. (HE PUTS THE CHAIR DOWN)

WILSON   Now then, gently sit down, sir. (HE LOWERS MAIN INTO THE CHAIR)

MAIN   Ow! Get me up, it's agony, I must stand. (WILSON PULLS HIM UP AGAIN)

JONES   What about brown paper and a hot iron, sir?

MAIN   (GASPING) As long as I stay like this, I'm all right. Just let me walk up and down for a bit.

(STILL BENT DOUBLE HE STARTS TO WALK UP AND DOWN. CAPT. OGILVIE ENTERS, HE

The whole crew, looking very young, on the churchyard set where Mainwaring conducted his PT exercises.

IS A TOUGH SCOT).

CAPT   Which is Capt. Mainwaring?

MAIN   I'm Capt. Mainwaring.

CAPT   (SALUTING) Oh! Capt. Ogilvie, Highland Regiment.

MAIN   (RETURNING THE SALUTE) How do you do. (HE SHAKES HANDS)

CAPT   Are you in some sort of trouble Capt.?

WILSON   Well you see, sir, it's his lumbago, he was showing us an exercise and he got stuck.

CAPT   Oh, is that all? I'll soon fix that, now hold still.

(HE GRIPS MAIN IN A HALF NELSON, PUTS HIS KNEE IN HIS BACK AND GIVES A QUICK JERK. MAIN OPENS HIS MOUTH, BUT NO SOUND COMES OUT.)

    There, how's that?

(MAIN MOUTHS 'ALL RIGHT')

CAPT   Good, then let's get down to business.

MAIN   (IN A FAINT VOICE) Fall the men in, Sgt.

WILSON   Right, fall in, men. (THEY DO SO)

CAPT   Now, Captain, I want you and your men to pay very careful attention, this is the scheme. A sergeant and nine of my men will attempt to capture your headquarters. We shall start from our H.Q. at Manor Farm which is three miles away, we will then infiltrate through the town and try to capture your H.Q. here. As you out-number us three to one, you shouldn't find it very difficult to stop us. On the other hand, my men are highly trained professional soldiers, one hundred per cent fit, (HE GLARES AT MAIN) so watch out for yourselves. Now each side will have three lots of paint. Red paint for dead, blue paint for wounded and white paint for a prisoner, they will then daub the enemy with the appropriate colour. If one of the enemy is wounded and taken prisoner as well, then you will daub him with a dash of blue and white paint. In the event of a dispute, you will call me, I shall be carrying a tin of orange and a tin of yellow paint. If I decide that he is wounded and not dead, I shall add one daub of orange paint. If on the other hand I think he is dead instead of wounded, I shall add two daub's of orange paint, but if I think that he is neither dead, wounded or a prisoner, I shall give him a daub of yellow paint which will cancel the whole thing.

(HE RATTLES THIS WHOLE SPEECH OFF AT A TERRIFIC SPEED)

Operations commence at 22.00 hrs. Now are there any questions?

(MAINWARING IS DOING FRANTIC SUMS ON HIS FINGERS, WILSON OPENS AND CLOSES HIS HAND TWICE TO SIGNAL TEN O'CLOCK. THE CAPTAIN IS LOOKING AT THE MEN AND DOES NOT SEE ALL THIS)

MAIN   (SUDDENLY) Ten o'clock.

CAPT   (FIERCELY) That's what I said, 22.00 hrs. If you want to see me I shall be at my H.Q. at Manor Farm. You can carry on with your P.T. now, Capt. Mainwaring, and I must say by the look of your men, they can do with it.

MAIN   They're pretty fit you know, sir.

CAPT   Really. (CROSSING TO PIKE) How old are you lad?

PIKE   17, sir.

CAPT   In another year or so you'll be ready for the army.

PIKE   I want to go into the navy, sir.

CAPT   You're very puny looking for your age, lad, and round shouldered too.

PIKE   I'm very fit, sir.

CAPT   Are you now? We'll just see how fit you are, now clench your stomach muscles tight. I'm just going to give you a 'wee' blow to test you. Are you ready?

(PIKE SCREWS HIS FACE UP TIGHT AND NODS. THE CAPT. GIVES HIM A NASTY LITTLE JAB WITH HIS RIGHT, THERE IS A THUD AND THE CAPT. DOUBLES UP WITH AGONY)

PIKE   How's that, sir?

CAPT   (GRITTING HIS TEETH) Splendid, that will be all Capt. Mainwaring, carry on.

(MAIN SALUTES. THE CAPTAIN DOES HIS BEST TO RETURN THE SALUTE WITH HIS INJURED HAND AND GOES)

MAIN   Good gracious, you took that well, Pike, anyone would think your stomach muscles were made of steel.

PIKE   It's not my stomach muscles, sir, it's my rifle bolt. (HE REACHES DOWN INTO HIS VEST AND PULLS OUT HIS BOLT)

FADE.

SCENE 3.

YARD OUTSIDE THE CHURCH HALL THE NEXT EVE.

THE MEN ARE DRAWN UP ON PARADE. MAIN IS ADDRESSING THEM.

MAIN   Now then, men, as Capt. Ogilvie told you yesterday, on the night manoeuvres on Saturday, he and nine of his best men are going to attempt to capture our Headquarters here. Now I don't mind telling you, we are up against a pretty formidable opponent. Now, are there any suggestions as to how we should tackle this problem?

FRAZER   Well, sir, there's one thing that's worrying me.

MAIN   What's that, Frazer?

FARZER   I feel a bit of a traitor, sir.

MAIN   How's that?

FRAZER   Well you see, sir, I'm a Highlander as well and I feel I'm fighting my own kith and kin, so to speak.

MAIN   Don't be absurd, Frazer, they're only acting the part of the enemy. After all, we're all British. I mean if Jerry comes out it won't make any difference whether you're wearing a kilt or trousers, he'll try to kill you just the same.

WALKER   On the other hand, if it's a dark night and you're wearing a kilt he might get other ideas.

JONES   Permission to speak, sir.

MAIN   Yes, Jones.

JONES   Well, sir, they're going to try and capture our headquarters, right.

(MAIN NODS)

Well why don't we move the headquarters, then when they get here they won't know where it is.

MAIN   I don't think that's quite the idea, Jones.

WILSON   I know, sir, why don't we send someone into the enemy's camp, so to speak, to find out what their plans are.

WALKER   That's a good idea, sir, all we've got to do is dress Frazer up to look like a Scotsman.

FRAZER   I am a Scotsman.

GODFREY   As it's a farm, sir, why not dress someone up as a landgirl.

MAIN   With all these soldiers about, Godfrey, it might have the wrong results.

WALKER   It's perfectly simple, sir, all we've got to do is disguise ourselves as something that won't look out of place on a farm.

MAIN   And what do you suggest, Walker.

WALKER   Leave it to me, sir.

FADE.

SCENE 4.
YARD. A LITTLE LATER.

WALKER AND FRAZER ARE DRESSED UP IN A PANTOMIME COW SKIN. THEY ARE STANDING IN FRONT OF THE PLATOON.

MAIN   It won't work, Walker.

(COW TURNS ITS HEAD TOWARDS MAIN)

I said it won't work. Oh, for goodness sake, take that stupid head off, Walker.

(WALKER STANDS UPRIGHT AND TAKES OFF THE HEAD)

MAIN   I wish you'd use your intelligence, Walker. How could you possibly pass for a real cow?

WALKER   No, sir, you don't understand. My plan is to get amongst a group of other cows.

MAIN   It still wouldn't work. All right, men – fall in inside the hall – put that thing back in the choir-room. You'd no business to touch it. (TO WILSON AS THEY GO) The vicar would be furious if he found out. He practically lives for that scout pantomime. *Jack and the Beanstalk* this year, isn't it?

WILSON   Yes, I must say, his reverence does make a simply marvellous dame.

MAIN   Hmm – a bit too lifelike for my money. (THEY GO)
(FRAZER'S HEAD POKES UP. HE IS THE REAR OF THE COW)

FRAZER   What did he say?

WALKER   Oh, the usual, he says it wouldn't work.

FRAZER   Well, how can we find out if we don't try?

WALKER   That's the spirit 'Tof'. Look, I tell you what, I'll come down to your shop tomorrow night about half past five . . .

TELECINE.

5. COW TROTTING ALONG COUNTRY LANE.
6. COW LOOKING ROUND CORNER OF FARM BUILDING.
7. COW TROTS UP TO GATE IN FIELD, HAND COMES OUT FROM SKIN, OPENS GATE, COW GOES THROUGH GATE, HAND COMES OUT AGAIN AND CLOSES GATE.
8. COW IN FIELD TROTS TOWARD BUNCH OF REAL COWS, IT GETS IN AMONGST THEM, KNEELS DOWN CROSSED LEGGED, HAND WITH A TELESCOPE COMES OUT OF SKIN. THE TELESCOPE PANS ROUND THE FIELD.
9. FARM HAND STARTS TO DRIVE COWS ACROSS FIELD. PANTO COW FOLLOWS, DOG BARKS AND SNAPS AT IT'S HEELS, COW KICKS AT DOG.
10. COW TROTTING ACROSS FIELD, SOUND OF A BULL, COW LOOKS ROUND, STARTS TO RUN, MORE BELLOWS.
FADE

Naturally, Walker and Frazer were not actually in the cow skin. Most people think that 'working' an animal skin is easy, but it is an art in itself. We used a professional double act, the Lynton Boys, to work the skin and they got the last ounce of comedy out of this sequence, particularly when the herd of real cows gathered round them and became curious.

'Now pay attention, men!' Captain Mainwaring briefs the platoon for *Operation Kilt*. As this photograph was taken during a rehearsal, Arthur Lowe is wearing his own glasses rather than Captain Mainwaring's pair.

SCENE 11.
YARD. THE NEXT EVENING.

THERE IS A LARGE BLACKBOARD WITH A MAP DRAWN ON IT. MAINWARING HAS A POINTER. THE REST OF THE MEN ARE STANDING AROUND.

MAIN Now, this is a rough plan of our position. Here is our H.Q. (HE POINTS) The enemy can either come in form the north, here. Through the Botanical Gardens or through the woods. Now, he won't come through the woods because if he does, he's got to cross this main road and we shall spot him at once. On the other hand, he can't get through the woods on to the beach because of the steep cliffs. So he'll either come in from the north through the Botanical Gardens or from the west.

WILSON   It's going to be a bit of a job to cover all these points with only 17 men.

(WALKER AND FRAZER ENTER WEARING THE REMAINS OF THE COW SKIN)

WALKER   You were right, sir, it didn't work.

MAIN   What happened?

WALKER   Well, sir, we got up close to the farm and we were doing really well, then we crossed the field.

MAIN   You mean someone spotted you.

WALKER   Yes, sir, a bull. He was in the field as well.

FRAZER   It was a terrible experience, sir.

WALKER   It wasn't as bad as all that.

MAIN   Well, Walker, I'll leave you to explain to the vicar how you ruined his cow skin. Now where was I, Wilson?

WILSON   We'd come to the conclusion we hadn't got enough men to go round, sir.

MAIN   You're right, Wilson, we must find some way of getting into that farm. Now we must keep cool and think. What examples can we take from great military campaigns of the past? For instance, what position would Napoleon take?

JONES   (STICKING HIS HAND IN HIS JACKET) He usually stood like this, sir.

MAIN   Thank you, Jones, I'm well aware of how Napoleon stood.

WILSON   What about the Trojan Horse, sir?

MAIN   The Trojan Horse.

WILSON   Yes, you see what I have in mind is this ...

FADE.

SCENE 12.
YARD LATER.

A SMALL TRACTOR WITH A TRUCK LOADED WITH HAY IS DRAWN UP.

MAIN   Well done, Wilson, how on earth did you manage to get this so quickly?

WILSON   It came from Mr Gregg's farm.

MAIN   Oh yes, I know him, he banks with us.

WILSON   That's right, sir.

MAIN   Well?

WILSON   Well, you know he asked you for an overdraught and you refused?

MAIN   Yes.

WILSON   Well I told him you'd changed your mind.

MAIN   You'd no right to exceed your authority like that, Wilson.

WILSON   I'm sorry, sir.

MAIN   Well, now we've got it, we might as well use it. Now we want someone to hide in the straw, then we drive it into the yard at Manor Farm and leave it there.

27

JONES   (RUSHING FORWARD) Permission to speak, sir. I'll do that.

MAIN   I think perhaps we ought to have a younger man. Pike, you'd better do it and as you brought it here, Wilson, you'd better drive it. The trouble is they'll recognise you at once.

WILSON   No they won't, sir, excuse me a minute. (HE GOES)

MAIN   All right, Pike, get under the straw.

PIKE   But, sir, I ...

MAIN   Don't argue, boy, do as I say. Come on, Godfrey, Frazer, lend a hand.

(THEY ALL PUSH PIKE UNDER THE STRAW)

MAIN   There, that should do the trick.

(SUDDENLY FROM UNDER THE STRAW THERE ARE THREE HUGE SNEEZES YOUNG PIKE BURSTS OUT WITH HIS NOSE AND EYES STREAMING)

What on earth's the matter with you, boy?

PIKE   (WITH HIS FACE BURIED IN A HANDKY) I keep trying to tell you, Mr Mainwaring, it's my hayfever. (HE GIVES ANOTHER TERRIBLE SNEEZE)

JONES   (RUSHING FORWARD AGAIN) Permission to speak, sir. Let me go in, sir.

MAIN   Oh all right, Jones, seeing as you're so keen. Wait a minute, how are you going to breathe?

GODFREY   What about a length of rubber tubing, sir.

MAIN   An excellent idea, Godfrey, go into the hall and get the stirrup pump.

(GODFREY EXITS)

MAIN   All right now, come on, you men, get him under the straw.

(GODFREY ENTERS WITH PUMP)

GODFREY   Here you are, Mr Mainwaring.

MAIN   Thank you, Godfrey (HE PULLS THE HOSE OFF THE PUMP) Here you are, Jones, stick this in your mouth.

(BUSINESS GETTING JONES INTO STRAW)

That should be all right.

(WILSON ENTERS DRESSED IN SMOCK, FELT HAT AND FARMER GILES BEARD)

Where did you get all that stuff, Wilson?

WILSON   The same place as they got the cow skin from.

MAIN   I don't know what the vicar's going to say, I'm sure. Now listen, if you're challenged, don't say anything. Just shake your head and say Ahhh!

WILSON   All right, sir, I know.

MAIN   Well go on, try it.

WILSON   Ahhhh!

MAIN   I suppose that will have to do. (HE ADDRESSES THE CART) Now listen to me,

Jones, I want you to keep your eyes open, and remember everything you hear, do you hear that?

JONES   (SILENCE)

MAIN   Jones, can you hear me? (HE PICKS UP THE TUBE AND SHOUTS DOWN IT)

WILSON Jones. (HE PULLS THE TUBE AND IT COMES AWAY) He's got no air, sir, he'll suffocate. Quick get all that straw off the cart.

(THEY ALL TEAR THE STRAW OFF THE CART. WHEN THE CART IS EMPTY THERE IS STILL NO SIGN OF JONES)

MAIN   Oh, for goodness sake, where is he?

(JONES TAPS MAIN ON SHOULDER)

MAIN   Jones, where have you been?

JONES   I fell through the bottom of the cart.

FADE

SCENE 13.

TELECINE

FARM YARD. HAY CART AND TRACTOR ARE STANDING IN THE MIDDLE OF THE YARD. CLOSE UP OF TOP OF JONES'S HEAD POKING THROUGH THE TOP OF HAY. CLOSE UP OF CLOCK ON STABLE AT NINE. CLOSE UP OF CLOCK AT TWELVE. VOICE 'ALL NIGHT MANOEUVRE SECTION OVER HERE'. SOUND OF RUNNING FEET JONES'S HEAD BOBS DOWN.

CAPT   All right, Sgt., fix the plan on the back of the cart here.

(SGT. FIXES LARGE PLAN ON CART)

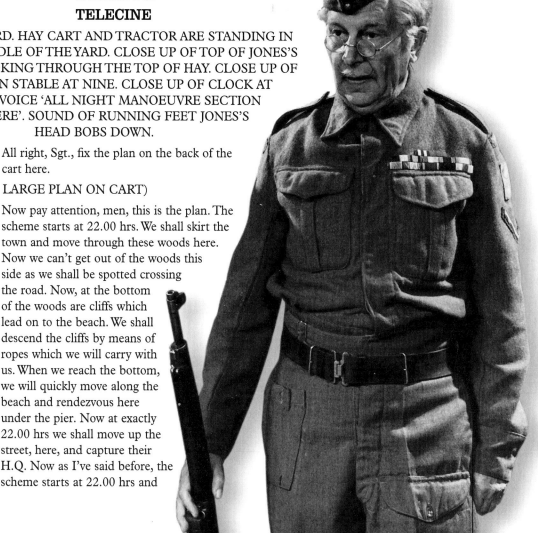

Now pay attention, men, this is the plan. The scheme starts at 22.00 hrs. We shall skirt the town and move through these woods here. Now we can't get out of the woods this side as we shall be spotted crossing the road. Now, at the bottom of the woods are cliffs which lead on to the beach. We shall descend the cliffs by means of ropes which we will carry with us. When we reach the bottom, we will quickly move along the beach and rendezvous here under the pier. Now at exactly 22.00 hrs we shall move up the street, here, and capture their H.Q. Now as I've said before, the scheme starts at 22.00 hrs and five minutes later we shall be in their H.Q. here. (HE STICKS A FLAG WITH A LARGE PIN) and here (HE STICKS IN ANOTHER FLAG. CLOSE UP OF JONES'S FACE SCREWED UP IN AGONY)

FADE.

SCENE 14.

WOODS – NIGHT.

MAIN AND WILSON ARE COVERED WITH FOLIAGE.

WILSON   I only hope this idea of yours works, sir.

MAIN   Well it worked all right in the Tarzan film I saw. The dirty rotters starting an hour early.

WILSON   Well, all's fair in love and war, sir, besides, they're only getting into position a little earlier. I mean, they're not going to move off from their rendezvous until 22.00 hrs.

MAIN   Well, they won't even get into their rendezvous if I have anything to do with it.

(JONES ENTERS WITH THE REST OF THE PLATOON)

JONES   We've got all the paint, sir.

MAIN   Thank you, Jones, now pay attention, men. I'll just go over our plan again. Now there are eight paths through the woods and every one is covered by a man trap. Now what happens is this. The enemy comes running down the path, he puts his foot in that noose, the counterweights take his weight, then one of you pulls the rope and then up he goes, feet first.

FRAZER   Excuse me, sir, have you ever seen it work?

MAIN   Of course I've seen it work. I er …

WILSON   He saw it work in a Tarzan film.

WALKER   'Ere, what about this paint then, sir?

MAIN   Oh yes, now it's red for wounded.

WILSON   No, sir, it's red for dead, blue for wounded.

JONES   No, no, you've got it all wrong, Mr Wilson. It's white for wounded, and yellow for dead.

PIKE   Why don't we give them a bit of each, sir, just to make sure?

MAIN   Splendid idea, Pike. Initiative, that's what I like to see.

PIKE   I saw it in a Laurel and Hardy film, sir.

MAIN   There's just one little point, men, about this paint. Standing orders state that during manoeuvres marking paint will not be put on uniforms.

WALKER   Where do we put it then, sir?

MAIN   On the boots. In this way, it can easily be wiped off.

During the war, the cinema and radio were the only sources of entertainment, as there was no television. Young Pike would have 'gone to the pictures' at least two or three times a week. A small town would have boasted at least four cinemas and there would have been queues outside them all. People were constantly quoting films and talking about them.

FRAZER But if they're hanging upside down with their feet in the air, how are we going to reach their boots?

JONES Permission to speak, sir.

MAIN Yes, Jones.

JONES Why don't we tie brushes on the end of long poles, then we'll be able to reach their boots?

MAIN I'm afraid that would waste too much time. We'll just have to put the paint on their hands or face. (LOOKING AT WATCH) All right, now, we've got another hour before they're due, so take up your positions. Walker, Jones, you will remain here to man this path. All right, move out, and the best of luck.

(THEY ALL GO. WALKER AND
JONES ARE LEFT ALONE)

When the platoon left the confines of the church hall, it would often be at night. Dimming the lights for night shots in the studio helped to conceal the shortcomings of the scenery.

Filming outdoors was always kept to a minimum due to the expense. Note the modest size of the film unit here – one camera and only one light.

WALKER	'Ere, Jonesy, I've just thought of something.
JONES	What's that?
WALKER	Well, there's eight man traps and ten men attacking, right?
JONES	Yes.
WALKER	That means we haven't got enough man traps.
JONES	You're right, Joe.
WALKER	Look, we've got plenty more rope. Let's rig up another just to make sure.
JONES	Good idea.
WALKER	All right, go and get the rope.
JONES	You go and get the rope, mate. (POINTS TO STRIPE) What do you think this is, Scotch mist?

FADE.

SCENE 15.

WOODS - NIGHT.

JONES AND WALKER ARE JUST PUTTING THE FINISHING TOUCHES
TO THE 2ND TRAP.

JONES   There, that should do the trick. Come on, let's hide ourselves, they'll be here in a minute.

(THEY PULL THE BUSHES ROUND THEM AND SETTLE DOWN)

(OWL HOOTS, FULL MOON AND CLOUDS RACING ACROSS THE SKY. BACK TO JONES AND WALKER)

JONES   'Ere, Joe.

WALKER   What?

JONES   Can you hear anything?

WALKER   No.

JONES   Neither can I.

WALKER   What are you talking about, you silly old buffer?

JONES   Well, I thought perhaps you could hear something that I couldn't hear.

WALKER   Well I can't.

(SUDDENLY A WHISTLE GOES, FOLLOWED BY LOUD SHOUTS)

JONES   Blimey, they're here, stand by, Joe.

(DEAD SILENCE)

They've gone a bit quiet.

(THERE IS A SWISHING SOUND AND A CRY)

That's the first trap. (HE CHALKS ON A TREE) (TWO MORE CRIES) Number two and three. (HE MARKS THE TREE) (MORE CRIES) Four, five, six, seven. (HE MARKS THE TREE) We're next, stand by.

(SILENCE)

WALKER   Perhaps they've taken the wrong turning.

JONES   Shush! I'm trying to listen.

(MAIN AND WILSON COME THROUGH THE BUSHES)

MAIN   Good night's work, men.

(JONES TURNS WITH A START)

JONES   Oh it's you, Mr Mainwaring, you did give me a start.

MAIN   What's happened?

WALKER   Nothing yet, sir.

(FRAZER ENTERS)

FRAZER   We've got all the men taken prisoner, sir.

MAIN   Quiet, Frazer, we're still waiting for the others.

WILSON   Perhaps they don't know where the trap is, sir.

33

MAIN   Well, of course he doesn't know where the trap is, I mean if he knew where it was he wouldn't run into it, would he?

JONES   Permission to speak, sir.

MAIN   Yes, Jones.

JONES   Look, why don't I go out there, sir, and get him to chase me, then I can lead him into the trap.

MAIN   Good idea, Jones.

JONES   Right, sir, and if two figures come crashing through the bushes, let the first one go by; that will be me.

MAIN   Right, off you go, Jones, and good luck.

(JONES GOES)

There's no doubt about it, that man's got guts, Wilson.

WILSON   Yes, sir, very gutty.

MAIN   All right, get your paint brushes ready, men. (THEY DIP THEIR BRUSHES IN THE PAINT AND WAIT) And keep the paint off the uniform. (THERE ARE LOUD SHOUTS) Stand by, men, here they come, and don't forget to let Jones go by first.

(THE FIRST FIGURE CRASHES ACROSS THE PATH AND INTO THE BUSHES. HE IS FOLLWED BY THE SECOND FIGURE)

All right, men, pull.

(THE SECOND FIGURE FLIES IN THE AIR. FRAZER AND WALKER SLOSH PAINT ON HIS FACE)

Stop! It's Jones.

WILSON   I don't understand at all, sir, who was the first man?

CAPT   That was me. (THEY ALL SPIN ROUND, THE CAPT. IS STANDING BEHIND THEM WITH A TOMMY GUN)

I must congratulate you, Capt. Mainwaring, you almost outsmarted us.

MAIN   Really, sir, I must protest.

CAPT   Don't. I'm afraid it's red paint on the boots for all. Right line up. (TO FRAZER) All right, hand me that brush and red paint; wait a minute, on second thoughts, I'll get it myself.

(HE STEPS FORWARD AND PUTS HIS BOOT IN THE SECOND NOOSE, HE FLIES UP IN THE AIR AND HANGS UPSIDE DOWN WITH HIS KILT HANGING OVER HIS FACE. CLOSE–UP OF MAIN AND WILSON. THEY QUICKLY PUT THEIR HANDS OVER THEIR EYES THEN THEY SLOWLY OPEN THEIR FINGERS)

WILSON   Good lord, sir.

MAIN   Yes, Wilson, now we really know what they wear underneath.

END.

DAD'S ARMY NO. 8

The Battle of Godfrey's Cottage

CAST

Capt. George Mainwaring.	Arthur Lowe
Sgt. Arthur Wilson	John Le Mesurier
L/Cpl. Jack Jones.	Clive Dunn
Pte. James Frazer	John Laurie
Pte. Joe Walker.	James Beck
Pte. Charles Godfrey	Arnold Ridley
Pte. Frank Pike	Ian Lavender
Mrs Pike.	Janet Davis
Dolly.	Amy Dalby
Cissy	Nan Brauton
A.R.P. Warden	Bill Pertwee
Pte. Sponge	Colin Bean
Remainder of Platoon	Richard Jacques
	Frank Godfrey
	Alec Coleman
	Hugh Cecil
	Jimmy Mac
	Desmond Callum-Jones
	Vic Taylor
	David Seaforth
	Richard Kitteridge

A Confrontation With The Cast

When David and I were writing this second series, we had no hint of the great success the show would finally become. The critical reaction had been lukewarm for the first series and, consequently, we had no idea how the second series would be received. A small article in the TV section of an up-market newspaper said, 'The BBC have commissioned a second series of the rather lightweight comedy *Dad's Army*. In spite of its charm, with its feeble jokes and obvious characters, it hardly got off the ground the first time round. Let's hope in the next series the writers can pull something original out of the bag and give it some depth.'

All comedy writers feel insecure until a show takes off, and reading an article like that hardly gave us confidence. In spite of this, David and I approached rehearsals with a certain amount of confidence. We knew that the show was good, but were slightly apprehensive about the way the actors were tackling their characters. For instance, was Bill Pertwee playing the warden too much over the top? Was John Le Mesurier as Sergeant Wilson too laid back? Clive Dunn as Corporal Jones was supposed to be the same age as John Laurie and Arnold Ridley, but they were both in their seventies and he was only in his late forties. In spite of the fact that Clive wore a white wig and moustache, would it look right beside two 'real' old men? Recently, Clive, who lives in Portugal, was in London to attend a function to celebrate the thirtieth anniversary of *Dad's Army*, and I said to him, 'Clive, now you look the right age to play Corporal Jones!'

One of our big worries was Arthur Lowe. Although when it came to the recording in the studio he was magnificent, it was a struggle to get him to learn his lines during rehearsals. To be fair to Arthur, I think this was because, like me, he had done years of weekly rep (performing a new play every week), and he hated learning lines. It was during the rehearsals of this script, 'The Battle of Godfrey's Cottage', that things came to a head. Our production manager was a young man named Harold Snoad. Harold was as sharp as a razor. I always called him 'the bravest man I know' because at the tea break he didn't mince matters and said to the cast, 'Let's face it, some of you do not know your lines well enough,' which was quite true, of course. There was a terrible silence, my blood froze, and the cast stared at Harold dumbfounded. They were a bunch of tough old pros, and it was the first time that anyone had had the courage to speak to them in that way. Would there be a terrible confrontation? They all stared at Harold in disbelief and then walked away muttering. It soon blew over and Harold Snoad became part and parcel of the show and worked amicably with the cast for quite a time, directing a number of episodes. Later, he and Michael Knowles adapted all the TV shows for radio, which became just as successful as the TV series.

Jimmy Perry

SCENES

1. OUTSIDE NOVELTY ROCK EMPORIUM
2. INSIDE NOVELTY ROCK EMPORIUM
3. OFFICE AT BANK
4. SIDE OFFICE CHURCH HALL
5. THE SITTING ROOM OF GODFREY'S COTTAGE
6. INSIDE THE NOVELTY ROCK EMPORIUM
7. GODFREY'S COTTAGE DUSK
8. THE REVOLVING SUMMER HOUSE AT THE BOTTOM OF GODFREY'S COTTAGE
9. INSIDE COTTAGE
10–15. SUMMER HOUSE / COTTAGE

SCENE 1.
OUTSIDE NOVELTY ROCK EMPORIUM.

THE FRONT OF THE SHOP IS SANDBAGGED IN, AND THE DOOR IS BOARDED OVER. THE NAME CAN STILL BE CLEARLY SEEN OVER THE SHOP.

SCENE 2.
INSIDE NOVELTY ROCK EMPORIUM.

CAPTAIN MAIN IS ALONE, HE IS JUST PUTTING THE FINISHING TOUCHES TO A LARGE DIAGRAM WHICH IS FIXED TO THE WALL.

HE GIVES A LITTLE BELCH, AND THUMPS HIS CHEST. THE SHOP BELL RINGS AND WILSON ENTERS PUSHING HIS BIKE.

WILSON   Good evening, sir, you're early.

MAIN   Yes, I wanted to finish this battle plan. (HE GIVES ANOTHER BELCH) Unfortunately, I had to rather rush my evening meal.

WILSON   Oh, what did you have tonight, sir?

MAIN   Woolton pie and treacle tart.

WILSON   You had a real meal, eh, sir. But how did you get the treacle?

MAIN   Well, it wasn't real treacle; it's a new recipe my wife was trying out. The pastry is made from potato, and the treacle from grated carrot and saccharin.

WILSON   What's it taste like?

MAIN   Terrible. (HE THUMPS HIS CHEST AGAIN)

WILSON   Indigestion, sir?

MAIN   Just a touch of flatulence.

WILSON   (HANDING HIM A LITTLE BOX) Try one of these, sir.

MAIN   Hmm! Sooth-ette tablets. Quick relief from all tummy upsets. Also combats air-raid strain. What's air-raid strain got to do with the tummy?

37

WILSON   Well, it can be a little embarrassing, you know, sir.

(SHOP BELL GOES AND JONES AND FRAZER COME IN BOTH PUSHING THEIR BIKES)

JONES   Evening, Mr Mainwaring, Mr Wilson.

(FRAZER NODS, MAIN SHAKES TWO TABLETS ONTO HIS HAND AND POPS THEM IN HIS MOUTH)

What's that you're taking, Mr Mainwaring? (HE LOOKS AT THE BOX) You shouldn't have taken those, you know.

MAIN   Why not?

JONES   Give you the runs, them do.

MAIN   Really, I thought they had the opposite effect.

JONES   Touch of wind, is it? 'Ere, try some of this.

(HE FISHES A LARGE MEDICINE BOTTLE OUT OF HIS PACK)

JONES   There you are, the old bicarbonate-of-soda. I always carry it with me, you know. Got into the habit when I was in the Sudan. General Kitchener was very keen on it. Boys, he used to say, always keep your bayonets sharpened and your bicarbonate-of-soda ready, then you won't get the wind up. He had a very dry, subtle sense of humour, you know, sir. That was forty-five years ago, sir, and I've always carried this bottle of bicarbonate ever since. Mind you, it's not the same lot.

MAIN   Thank you, Jones, but I think I'm all right now.

JONES   (PUTTING IT BACK IN HIS PACK) Well, if you want it, sir, just let me know.

FRAZER   It's going to be a bit crowded with the whole platoon in this wee shop, don't you think, Mr Mainwaring?

MAIN   It's only for this evening, Frazer, we shall just have to manage the best we can.

(THE SHOP BELL IS NOW GOING PRETTY HARD. AS THE REST OF THE PLATOON ARRIVE MOST OF THEM ARE PUSHING THEIR BIKES)

WILSON   Don't you think we ought to remove the shop bell, sir, it's a bit of a nuisance?

> **General Kitchener was rumoured to be a homosexual, and whenever he quoted him Corporal Jones put his hand on his hip. Clive Dunn did this quite by chance one day, and we kept it in the series.**

MAIN   Nuisance, where's your imagination, Wilson? It will stop the enemy taking us by surprise.

(THE SHOP IS NOW CROWDED OUT)

Oh really, Wilson, we can't have all these bikes in here. There won't be room to swing a cat. Tell them to put them outside.

WILSON   Would you mind putting your bikes outside, please?

MAIN   Give it as an order, Wilson. All bikes outside!! That goes for you too, Wilson, put your bike outside.

WILSON   Yes, sir. Shall I put yours out as well?

MAIN   No, wait a minute. On second thoughts, I think there's just room for two.

(WALKER ENTERS)

WALKER   Good evening, gents. What's this, are you turning it into a second-hand bicycle shop, Mr Mainwaring? By the way, here's the tin of treacle I promised you.

MAIN   Thank you, Walker. (THUMPING HIS CHEST) I could have done with that earlier.

(PIKE ENTERS PUSHING HIS BIKE)

(BY NOW, MOST OF THE PLATOON ARE OUTSIDE THE SHOP)

PIKE   Why are all the men leaving, Mr Mainwaring, is the parade over?

MAIN   It hasn't started yet, you stupid boy. I told them to put their bikes outside. You'd better put yours outside too.

PIKE   (TO WILSON) Mum's not going to like me

> Although Mainwaring was always saying how wrong it was to have anything to do with the black market, constant pressure from his wife Elizabeth forced him to deal with Walker.

leaving my bike in the street, you know, Uncle Arthur, it might get pinched. Anyhow, it's not fair: you and Mr Mainwaring have got yours in here.

MAIN   That will do, Pike, put your bike outside at once. (HE GOES PUSHING HIS BIKE) All right, Jones, fall the men in. Just a minute, Wilson, I want to talk to you.

JONES   Platoon fall in.

(THE MEN FALL IN. MAIN AND WILSON ARE TALKING RIGHT UP CLOSE AGAINST THE WALL. THEY HAVE THEIR BACKS TO THE PLATOON)

MAIN   (WHISPERING) Now look here, Wilson, I wish you'd stop young Pike calling you Uncle Arthur, it's bad for discipline, you know.

WILSON   I'm sorry, sir, it's not really my fault. You see, when he was a little boy he used to call me something else and Mavis, I mean Mrs Pike, told him to call me Uncle Arthur to stop him er ... calling me something else.

MAIN   What did he used to call you?

WILSON   (DROPPING HIS VOICE RIGHT DOWN) Daddy.

MAIN   What?

WILSON   (FRANTIC WITH EMBARRASSMENT, MOUTHS THE WORD 'DADDY')

MAIN   Well, you're not really his daddy, I mean his father, are you?

WILSON   Certainly not, sir.

(DURING THIS, JONES HAS BEEN FALLING THE PLATOON IN AND CHECKING THEM OFF)

MAIN   Well you'll just have to tell him that in future ...

(THE MEN OPEN ORDER AND PIN MAINWARING AND WILSON TO THE WALL)

        What are you doing, Jones?

JONES   I'm sorry, sir, I didn't realise the place was so small.

(THE FRONT ROW OF THE PLATOON ARE STANDING JAMMED UP AGAINST THE WALL)

MAIN   (SHOUTING) Well put them back.

JONES   Yes, sir, sorry, sir. (IN A PANIC) Platoon, about turn.

(THE PLATOON ABOUT TURN, THE FRONT ROW NOW HAVE THEIR BACKS TO THE WALL AND THE BACK ROW HAVE THEIR FACES TO THE WALL)

MAIN   Jones, pull yourself together.

JONES   Sorry, sir. Platoon! Close order, march.

(THEY DO SO. THEY ARE NOW FACING THE WRONG WAY ROUND)

MAIN   Put them in order, Wilson.

WILSON   Platoon, about turn.

MAIN   That's better. Who's missing, Jones?

JONES   Godfrey, sir.

MAIN   Oh well, we'll just have to carry on without him. All right, men, on the command, fall out. I want you to gather round the board here. Platoon, fall out!

(THEY ALL SIT IN A TIGHT CIRCLE AROUND THE BOARD)

        Now pay attention, men. This morning I received orders from G.H.Q. giving us our

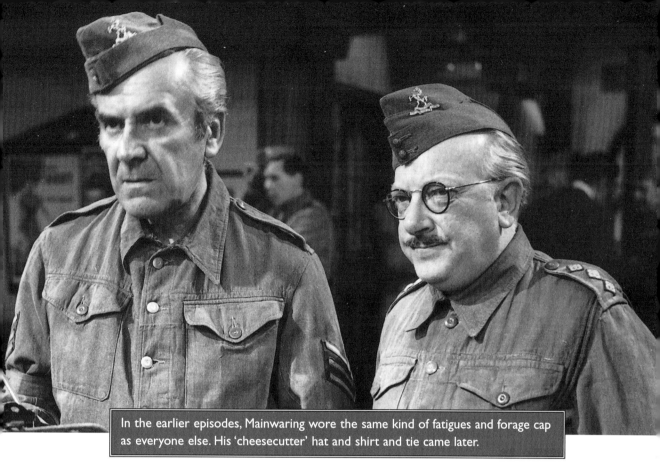

In the earlier episodes, Mainwaring wore the same kind of fatigues and forage cap as everyone else. His 'cheesecutter' hat and shirt and tie came later.

exact instructions in case the balloon goes up. Now, I've asked you to parade here tonight at the Novelty Rock Emporium because, in the event of an invasion, this shop will be our command post, our nerve centre.

(THE SHOP BELL GOES AND AN A.R.P. WARDEN COMES IN)

WARDEN   (STRIDING OVER TO THE MEN) Who's in charge here?

(HE GIVES WILSON A PUSH)

WILSON   (POINTING) Capt. Mainwaring.

WARDEN   Oh, it's you again, is it? What are all these bicycles doing outside?

MAIN   They belong to members of my platoon.

WARDEN   I don't care who they belong to; get 'em shifted.

MAIN   I don't think I like your tone.

WARDEN   Oh don't you? Then I'll try it in a different tone. Get 'em shifted. How's that?

MAIN   Don't you think you're rather exceeding your authority.

WARDEN   Section 4, paragraph 2 of the Defence of the Realm Act states, 'No vehicles or any other means of transport will be left unattended in a usable condition.' Don't you realise those bicycles could be used by enemy parachute troops?

MAIN   What er ... I am well aware of the situation, and I shall take steps to see that it is attended to.

WARDEN   You'd better, mate, otherwise I shall have to let the tyres down.

MAIN   Don't you dare lay a finger on those tyres. Now leave my shop, I mean my command post, at once.

WARDEN   I'm going, but don't say I haven't warned you.

(HE STEPS OVER THE MEN AND GOES)

MAIN   Cpl. Jones, detail a man to stand over those bicycles.

JONES   Yes, sir. (HE CROSSES TO EXTRA) Pte. Sponge, outside and stand guard over those bikes, fix your bayonet, and if that warden touches those tyres, let him have it right up.

(PTE. SPONGE GOES THROUGH THE DOOR AND JONES SHUTS IT AFTER HIM)

MAIN   Jones, lock the door. I don't want that warden tramping all over the platoon again.

(JONES LOCKS THE DOOR)

Now, men, as I was saying, in the event of an invasion, this is the plan.

(THERE IS A KNOCKING ON THE SHOP DOOR)

All right, leave this to me, men.

(HE STEPS OVER THE PLATOON AND UNLOCKS THE DOOR)

Now look here ... (IT IS GODFREY) Oh, it's you, Godfrey.

GODFREY   Are you closed?

MAIN   Why are you late, Godfrey?

GODFREY   (STILL OUTSIDE THE DOOR) I'm sorry, sir, my bicycle had a puncture so I had to walk.

MAIN   Well, don't stand out there, man, come in. (GODFREY COMES IN. MAIN LOCKS THE DOOR AND STEPS OVER THE PLATOON AND TAKES UP HIS POSITION BY THE BOARD) Now, as I was saying, as soon as you hear the church bells you will proceed at once to the Novelty Rock Emporium, here. (HE POINTS TO THE MAP) I shall then divide the platoon into two sections. I shall take half and Sgt. Wilson will take the other half. The first section will then move off to the crossroads, here, one mile away. Now, we need to establish a second command post, and I think the ideal place would be your cottage, here, Godfrey. You don't mind, do you?

GODFREY   Mind what, sir?

MAIN   If we use your cottage as a command post. You live with your two sisters, don't you?

GODFREY   That's right, sir, the trouble is they might be in bed when the invasion comes and, as they're a little hard of hearing, they might not hear us to let us in.

> This was before the ARP warden became a regular feature of the series. We based him on the many petty officials who achieved power because of the war. As the series progressed, we gave him the name Hodges and invented a greengrocer's shop for him to run. Later we made him a chief warden, and he wore a white steel helmet in which he gloried. In the last episode of the series he confessed to Mainwaring that he enjoyed every minute of the war, as it gave him the one thing he had always wanted – power! He was almost in tears when he said that if there hadn't been a war he would have just been an ordinary greengrocer.

The character of Hodges became more prominent as the show developed. There was always ample scope for him to come into conflict with Mainwaring.

MAIN   Well, you've got a key, haven't you?

GODFREY   Well, no, sir, you see there's only one and they've got it.

JONES   Permission to speak, sir. Why don't they leave it under a flower pot?

MAIN   Excellent idea, Jones, see to it, Godfrey. So that's the plan, men. (HE STOPS) Now from these two command posts (HE IS STARTING TO LOOK VERY UNCOMFORTABLE) we shall send out patrols and both (HE STARTS TO TALK

VERY QUICKLY) command posts will keep in touch by means of runners. (HISSING TO WILSON) Have you got a penny on you, Wilson?

WILSON   What on earth for?

MAIN   (DESPERATE) Don't argue, give it to me now.

(WILSON HANDS HIM A PENNY. HE SNATCHES IT AND RUSHES TO THE DOOR, TRIES TO PULL IT OPEN AND FINDS IT LOCKED)

I can't get out. (WILSON AND JONES CROSS TO THE DOOR)

JONES   Of course you can't: it's locked, sir.

MAIN   Well, unlock it then.

(JONES UNLOCKS DOOR AND MAIN RUSHES OUT)

JONES   (TO WILSON) I said he shouldn't have taken those tablets, you know.

FADE.

SCENE 3.
OFFICE AT BANK.

MAIN IS SITTING AT HIS DESK, MRS PIKE IS SITTING FACING HIM. THERE IS A NEWSPAPER ON THE DESK. C.U. OF HEADLINES '50 NAZI DIVISIONS POISED ACROSS CHANNEL'.

MAIN   Yes, I think we should definitely sell your Channel Tunnel shares, Mrs Pike, and buy some war loan, they seem to be going well. (HE PRESSES A BUTTON)

MRS PIKE   I'm so grateful for your advice, Mr Mainwaring. You see, being a widow, it's not always easy to know what to do for the best.

MAIN   I quite understand, Mrs Pike, but don't worry, as your bank manager, I'm always here to help.

MRS PIKE   You see, Mr Mainwaring, (WILSON COMES QUIETLY AND STANDS BESIDE MRS PIKE) what I miss most is having a man to look after. (SHE TURNS AND HER EYE IS IN LINE WITH WILSON'S JACKET) You've got a button missing, Arthur, why didn't you tell me before you left this morning?

WILSON   (ASIDE TO MRS PIKE) Mavis, please. You sent for me, sir?

MAIN   Yes, here is a list of Mrs Pike's shares. I want you to sell, (HANDS HIM LIST) Wilson. Anytime I'm not here, Mrs Pike, you'll find our chief clerk is perfectly well equipped to handle your affairs.

MRS PIKE   (BLUSHING, LOOKING DOWN) Yes, I'm sure. (GETTING UP) Well, I'd better 'Go to it'. Mr Wilson's coming to supper with me tonight, aren't you, Arthur.

MAIN   I'm afraid he won't be able to, Mrs Pike, he's taking a party of 18 to the cinema at Eastgate.

MRS PIKE   What?

WILSON   Home Guards.

Today we take the Channel Tunnel for granted, but thirty years ago, when this episode was written, it was an outlandish idea. Although several tunnelling companies had been formed over the years and a mile of it had been dug, it was regarded as a joke.

You never know who's listening!

CARELESS TALK COSTS LIVES

MAIN	It's a special showing for all H.G. units of the film *Next of Kin*.
MRS PIKE	*Next of Kin*, I've heard of that. Are you all going?
MAIN	Yes, except me. I took my wife and her two sisters to see it last week.
WILSON	Coals to Newcastle, eh, sir.
MRS PIKE	Goodbye, Mr Mainwaring. (WILSON CROSSES TO THE DOOR AND OPENS IT) Don't worry about your supper, Arthur. If you're late I'll warm it up for you, I've only got to bung it in the oven.
WILSON	Oh, Mavis, please. (SHE GOES)
MAIN	I don't want to pry into your private affairs, Wilson, but what did Mrs Pike say as she just left?
WILSON	My supper, sir, she's going to bung it in the oven.

MAIN   Oh, bung! I'm glad I'm not coming with you tonight, Wilson. I've got a lot of paperwork to catch up with down at H.Q. Well, I'm off now. I'll leave you to lock up. Oh, look, Mrs Pike's forgotten her gloves, run after her. (WILSON TAKES THE GLOVES AND GOES. MAIN PUTS ON HIS BOWLER HAT AND PICKS UP HIS TIN HAT AND GAS MASK. HE SEES A DEED BOX ON THE DESK) I'd better put Mrs Pike's deed box back in the vaults. (HE PICKS UP THE BOX AND OPENS THE DOOR TO THE VAULTS AND CLOSES IT BEHIND HIM. THE OFFICE DOOR OPENS, WILSON COMES IN)

WILSON   I just caught up with her in time ... Oh, he's gone, funny I didn't see him, I expect he left by the back door.

(PIKE ENTERS)

PIKE   The rest of the staff have gone, sir? Do you want me for anything else?

WILSON   No, that's all, Pike. I'll see you down at the coach. We haven't got much time, it leaves in 15 minutes.

PIKE   I can't understand why they're taking us all to the pictures tonight.

WILSON   G.H.Q. want all units to see the film. It deals with the effects of careless talk.

PIKE   Who's in it then?

WILSON   They didn't say. (CHURCH BELLS START TO RING) What's that?

PIKE   Church bells. Funny time of the day to ring them: perhaps someone's getting married.

WILSON   It's the invasion signal.

PIKE   Oh, Uncle Arthur, what are we going to do?

WILSON   Well, you can stop calling me Uncle Arthur for a start. We'd better get down to the Novelty Rock Emporium.

PIKE   But the coach is waiting to take us to the pictures.

To make Pike look even more gormless, the stitching which would normally hold his forage cap up in a neat peak was removed, allowing him to cram it down on his head.

WILSON	Well, we shall just have to go another night. Get your rifle and gas mask and I'll lock up. (HE GOES THROUGH THE DOOR)
PIKE	(FOLLOWING HIM THROUGH THE DOOR) But, Uncle Arthur, don't you think we ought to tell Mum ...

(HE CLOSES THE DOOR BEHIND HIM. THE CHURCH BELLS HAVE NOW STOPPED. THE DOOR FROM THE VAULT OPENS AND MAIN COMES BACK IN)

MAIN	(DUSTING HIMSELF OFF) Really, those deed boxes are in a terrible state down there. I must tell Wilson about it in the morning. (THERE IS THE SOUND OF THE FRONT DOOR OF THE BANK SLAMMING. MAIN GOES OUT OF THE DOOR INTO THE MAIN BANK.)
MAIN	Is that you, Wilson? Hmm, he didn't waste much time, must have thought I'd gone, and as soon as my back's turned he makes off. He's getting a bit of a clock watcher. I must have a word with him about that too in the morning.

FADE.

SCENE 4.
SIDE OFFICE CHURCH HALL.

MAIN IS SITTING AT HIS DESK. HE IS READING SOME PAPERS.

MAIN	(READING) To Officer Commanding 1st Platoon Walmington-on-Sea H.G. 'Subject Grenade Practice'. Dear sir, in light of the recent experience it has been found that the best thing to use as a dummy grenade is a knob from a brass bedstead, therefore, we suggest that you issue a memo to your platoon to supply as many brass bedstead knobs as they can lay their hands on. Yours sincerely, J. Roshe Brigadier etc. etc. Good idea, I'll put a notice on the board right away. (HE STARTS TO WRITE) Let me see now, heading 'BRASS KNOBS'. No, that's not right. (CROSSES IT OUT) Will all members of the platoon with brass knobs on their bedsteads please unscrew them and let me have them, this is urgent.

> **This was a real directive, and there really was a Brigadier J. Roshe.**

(THE DOOR BURSTS OPEN AND FRAZER AND JONES RUSH IN)

JONES	(GASPING FOR BREATH) Permission to speak, sir.
MAIN	What is it, Jones?
JONES	They're here, sir, we're just on our way to the Novelty Rock Emporium.
FRAZER	We just happened to see your bike outside as we were passing. Come on, sir, there's not a moment to lose.
MAIN	What are you talking about, Frazer?
FRAZER	The church bells, sir, they've been ringing.
MAIN	I've heard nothing. When was this?
FRAZER	About twenty minutes ago. I was at home having my tea so I went straight round to collect Jones at his house and we were just on our way to the command post.
MAIN	But this is terrible, the coach taking the rest of the platoon to the cinema will be half

way to Eastgate by now. We've been waiting for six months for this moment and now Hitler's at our throats and my platoon has gone to the pictures. By the way, why didn't you go with them?

JONES   Well, it's my coupon-counting night, sir.

FRAZER   And I was going to do my stock taking, but we've no time to argue about that now, sir. What are we going to do? There's only three of us left to defend the whole town.

MAIN   Just a minute, let me think.

JONES   (FIXING HIS BAYONET) We'll fight to the last, that's what we'll do, sir, fight to the last, and when we run out of ammo, we'll give them the old cold steel. They don't like it up 'em you see, sir, they don't like it up 'em.

MAIN   Oh, do pull yourself together, Jones.

JONES   Sorry, sir, it's just that I've got the smell of battle in me nostrils, it gets me going, you know. (HIS BAYONET IS SHAKING)

MAIN   Do put that away, Jones, you'll hurt someone.

FRAZER   It's going to be a bit difficult to defend the Novelty Rock Emporium with just three men, you know, sir.

John Laurie was in his seventies when *Dad's Army* began. Clive Dunn, on the other hand, was only in his forties. Make-up narrowed the age gap.

MAIN   You're right, Frazer. We shall have to change our plans, make a snap decision. A commander in the field must always be flexible. We'll go to the second command post, Godfrey's cottage. (HE CROSSES TO CUPBOARD AND UNLOCKS IT) That way we can defend the crossroads that lead into town.

(MAIN TAKES A LEWIS GUN OUT OF THE CUPBOARD)

MAIN   We'd better take this with us, Jones, Frazer, grab a magazine each.

JONES   I don't think we're going to have much time for reading, sir.

(FRAZER GRABS TWO MAGAZINE PANS AND GIVES ONE TO JONES)

FRAZER   Here.

JONES   Oh, I see.

MAIN   All right, men, at the double to Godfrey's cottage.

FADE.

> The Lewis light machine gun was used during World War I, especially in fighter planes. It fired a .303 calibre bullet and had a circular magazine which held 47 or 97 rounds. It was inclined to jam and was replaced by the far more efficient 'bren' gun. Due to the shortage of weapons, it was issued to the Home Guard, who became very proficient in overcoming its faults.

SCENE 5.
THE SITTING ROOM OF GODFREY'S COTTAGE.

OLDE WORLDE LATTICE WINDOWS. CHINTZ CURTAINS, PADDED CHAIRS AND A FRINGED PELMET ROUND THE MANTELPIECE. THE PLACE IS CROWDED WITH VICTORIAN KNIK-KNACKS. GODFREY IS SITTING HAVING HIS TEA WITH HIS TWO SISTERS, CISSY AND DOLLY. THEY ARE BOTH IN THEIR SEVENTIES. THERE IS A PARROT IN THE CORNER OF THE ROOM.
THEY ARE ALL THREE RATHER HARD OF HEARING.

DOLLY   Are you enjoying your nice bit of Haddock, Charles?

GODFREY   Yes, thank you, Dolly.

DOLLY   Do you know I had to queue up for twenty minutes this morning, just for a little bit of fish?

CISSY   Aren't you parading with the Yeomanry tonight, Charles?

GODFREY   No, dear, I have to go down to the clinic.

CISSY   Oh, I see you are; well you'd better hurry up or you'll be late for parade.

DOLLY   Don't rush him, Cissy, I'm sure he's got time for another cup of tea and one of my upside-down cakes. I made a fresh batch this afternoon. Mind you, I get so frustrated with the shortage of ingredients these days, my upside-down cakes are not what they were and, on top of that, when I went to take them out of the oven I found I'd put them in the wrong way up.

CISSY   That reminds me, have a little word with that nice Mr Walker tonight, will you, Charles? We need some more chocolate drops.

As the ingredients for upside-down cakes are pineapple, sugar, butter, glacé cherries and eggs — all of which were strictly rationed or completely unobtainable — it is difficult to imagine what ingredients the sisters used.

GODFREY But I'm not going on parade tonight, Cissy.

CISSY Thank you, dear, I'm sure he'll get them for you.

(GODFREY GIVES UP AND CARRIES ON EATING HIS TEA. THERE IS A LOUD SQUAWK FROM THE PARROT)

DOLLY (TO PARROT) What it is, Percy? Do you want your tea? How about a little of Cissy's upside-down cake? (SHE CRUMBLES SOME CAKE ON A SAUCER AND TAKES IT TO THE PARROT) Here you are, Percy.

PERCY Ger, you silly old faggot.

DOLLY No, no, it's not maggots, it's one of Cissy's upside-down cakes.

(THERE IS A LOUD KNOCKING AT THE DOOR. DOLLY GOES TO OPEN IT. THERE IS THE SOUND OF MUTTERING VOICES. SHE COMES BACK TO GODFREY)

Charles, dear, it's that nice bank manager Mr Mainwaring. He's got a big gun with him.

GODFREY I wonder what he wants. (HE QUICKLY CROSSES TO THE DOOR) Do come in, sir. (MAIN COMES INTO THE ROOM WITH JONES AND FRAZER).

MAIN What are you doing here, Godfrey? I thought you'd gone into Eastgate with the rest of the platoon.

GODFREY No, it's my night for clinic, sir.

FRAZER That makes one more of us anyhow, sir.

MAIN Well, hurry up and get your rifle and steel helmet: the invasion's on.

GODFREY What invasion, sir?

MAIN The Germans, of course, didn't you hear the church bells?

GODFREY No, sir, I'm afraid not.

MAIN There's no time to go into it all now; we're setting up our command post here. You did tell your sisters, didn't you?

GODFREY I'm afraid it slipped my mind, sir.

MAIN Well, you'd better tell them now. (LOOKING ROUND ROOM) We'll set the Lewis gun up here at this window. It gives us a clear line of fire. Give me a hand, Jones. (HE PUTS THE GUN ON DESK)

GODFREY Mind you don't scratch the top of that Regency desk, sir. (MAIN GIVES HIM A GLARE)

JONES What we really need at this window is some sandbags, sir.

FRAZER What about cushions and pillows, sir? If we could jam them round the window they'd give us some sort of protection.

MAIN Good idea, Frazer. Go round the house, get as many as you can.

(FRAZER GOES. THE ROOM IS NOW A HIVE OF ACTIVITY. MAIN AND JONES DRAG A SETTEE UP AGAINST THE WINDOW. THE TWO SISTERS ARE AT THE TABLE STILL SIPPING THEIR TEA)

DOLLY (TO GODFREY) Don't be so rude, Charles, offer your friends some tea.

GODFREY I don't think they want any just at the moment.

MAIN Come on, Godfrey, lend a hand.

GODFREY Yes, sir. (HE HAS NOW GOT HIS RIFLE AND IS PUTTING HIS STEEL HELMET ON)

CISSY It's that nice Mr Jones, the butcher from the high street.

DOLLY Would you like a cup of tea, Mr Jones?

JONES Not just now, thank you, the Misses Godfrey, you see the Germans are coming. (HE GETS BACK TO THE WINDOW)

DOLLY Yes, I know, so many people for tea. I think I'd better make some more.

(SHE TAKES THE TEAPOT AND GOES TO THE DOOR. AS SHE OPENS IT FRAZER COMES IN WITH AN ARMFUL OF CUSHIONS AND PILLOWS)

  Oh, good afternoon, there's a gentleman here selling pillows, Cissy. Just wait there will you, my sister will attend to you. (SHE GOES)

FRAZER Here you are, sir.

MAIN Well done, Frazer. (HE STARTS STACKING THEM IN THE WINDOW) Have a look round the room, see if you can find some more. (HE SEE THAT JONES IS STILL WEARING HIS STRAW HAT) Where's your helmet, Jones?

JONES Eh! (HE TAKES OFF HIS HAT) Oh blimey, sir, in all the confusion, I'm afraid I forgot it.

MAIN You must have a steel helmet, man.

GODFREY Wait a minute, Mr Mainwaring, I've got an idea. (HE REACHES OUT OF THE WINDOW. HE UNLOCKS AN OLD GERMAN STEEL HELMET WHICH IS HANGING UPSIDE DOWN WITH FLOWERS IN IT)

MAIN Thank you, Godfrey, but I don't think putting a flower pot on his head is going to help.

GODFREY It's not really a flower pot, sir, it's an old German steel helmet, I brought it back from France in 1918 as a souvenir.

MAIN It's better than nothing. (HE TAKES THE HELMET, EMPTIES THE FLOWERS AND EARTH OUT OF THE WINDOW) Sorry about your geraniums, Godfrey, but this is war. Here you are, Jones, put that on.

(JONES TAKES THE HELMET AND PUTS IT ON, THE WRONG WAY ROUND, THE NECKPIECE COVERS HIS EYES)

  You got it on the wrong way round, Jones.

JONES   (TURNING IT ROUND) Oh yes, sir, sorry, sir.

MAIN   Hurry up with the rest of the cushions, Frazer.

FRAZER   Coming, sir. (HE HAS GATHERED UP ALL THE CUSHIONS IN THE ROOM, EXCEPT THE ONE CISSY IS SITTING ON) Excuse me, Miss Godfrey, (HE TAKES THE CUSHION FROM UNDER HER. HE CROSSES TO THE WINDOW) Here you are, sir, that's the lot.

MAIN   (TAKING THE CUSHIONS) Well done, Frazer. Take up your position at the back window.

FRAZER   Ai, sir.

JONES   Oo er.

MAIN   What is it, Jones?

JONES   I've got a cold wriggly feeling down my spine, sir.

MAIN   Pull yourself together, Jones, you've been into action before.

JONES   Yes, but I've never had a cold wriggly feeling down my spine before. Ow. (HE SNATCHES OFF HIS HELMET AND PUTS HIS ARM DOWN HIS BACK INSIDE HIS SHIRT. HE PULLS OUT A WORM)

CISSY   (COMING INTO PICTURE) Well, if you will wear a flower pot on your head, what else can you expect, Mr Jones?

FADE.

SCENE 6.
INSIDE THE NOVELTY ROCK EMPORIUM.

WALKER AND WILSON ARE LOOKING UP THE STREET THROUGH
SLITS IN THE SANDBAGS.

WILSON   I don't like it, Walker, it's too quiet.

WALKER   It's funny you should say those words like that, Sarge.

WILSON   Oh, why?

WALKER   Well, that's what sergeants always say in those western films.

WILSON   Really.

WALKER   Yeh, you see this cavalry patrol are trotting along, they stop and the officer looks round through his field glasses. Then the sergeant says, I don't like it, sir, it's too quiet.

WILSON   Then what happens?

WALKER   He gets a dirty big arrow in his chest.

WILSON   (RAISING HIS EYEBROWS) I see.

WALKER   Mind you, sometimes it's the officer who say's it's too quiet.

WILSON   Then, I suppose he gets the arrow in his chest.

WALKER   No, the sergeant still gets the arrow. You see, the officer is always played by a big star and you can't have someone like Errol Flynn dying in the first reel, can you? No, the sergeant is definitely the first one to get it, thuck, right in the chest.

WILSON   All right, Walker, that will do.

WALKER   Here's young Pike.

'The Germans are coming, Miss Godfrey.'
'Yes, I know, so many people for tea. I think I'd better make some more.'

(THE SHOP BELL RINGS AND PIKE COMES IN WITH TWO EXTRAS)

WILSON	Well, where's the Lewis gun, Pike?
PIKE	It's not there, sir.
WILSON	What do you mean, not there!
PIKE	Well, Sarge, we went back to the Church Hall to fetch it like you told us, and when we got there the cupboard was open and the gun gone.
WALKER	Blimey, perhaps the Germans have taken it, Sarge.
WILSON	They wouldn't know where it was. I can't understand what's happened to Capt. Mainwaring and the rest of the platoon.
PIKE	Mr Frazer was the Lewis gunner, Sarge, wherever he is he's probably taken the gun with him.
WALKER	If he's gone where I think he's gone, he couldn't have taken it with him, son.
WILSON	Oh, go and stand somewhere else, Walker, you're getting on my nerves.
WALKER	There's not many places I can stand with all these flippin' bikes in here. (HE SLIDES OUT OF THE PICTURE)

(WILSON PEERS OVER THE SANDBAGS LOOKING UP THE STREET)

PIKE	Uncle Arthur, I mean, Sarge. Do you think Mr Mainwaring and the others are all right?

By now we were starting to plant the idea that Pike might be Wilson's son. We gave him some of Wilson's mannerisms, such as pulling at his right earlobe.

WILSON   Yes, of course they are.

PIKE   Well, why aren't they here, then? I mean Mr Mainwaring knows where to come, I mean, he told us. He said if you hear the church bells, go at once to the Novelty Rock Emporium.

WILSON   Oh, do be quiet, Pike. I'm trying to think. (SILENCE)

PIKE   Uncle Arthur?

WILSON   What is it now?

PIKE   I ain't half hungry.

WILSON   Well, you should have brought some sandwiches; you knew we were going over to Eastgate.

PIKE   Well, I thought I'd get an ice-cream in the pictures and have my supper when I got in.

(SILENCE)

PIKE   Uncle Arthur?

WILSON   What?

PIKE   If anything happens to Mr Mainwaring, will they make you the manager?

WILSON   (BRIGHTENING SLIGHTLY) I don't know, I hadn't thought about it.

PIKE   If they make you manager, perhaps they'll make me the chief clerk.

(WALKER COMES INTO THE PICTURE WITH A CARDBOARD BOX)

WALKER   'Ere, look what I've found down in the basement. (HE PULLS OUT SOME STICKS OF ROCK) They must have been there since before the war, shall I hand them out, Sarge. The platoon look as if they could do with a bit of nourishment.

WILSON   Yes, all right, Walker.

One of the main brands of ice cream sold during the war was Eldorado. What it was made of one could only guess, but to us they tasted delicious.

WALKER	Line up lads, get your rock 'ere, Walmington-on-Sea stamped right through it.
PRIVATE	How much?
WALKER	Eh! Oh, give me what you like, a spruzy will do. (HE TAKES MONEY)
PRIVATE	'Ere, this has got Clacton stamped on it.
WALKER	Well, what do you expect for a tanner, Ashby-de-la-Zouche?
WILSON	Walker, what are you doing taking money for that rock?
WALKER	Sorry, Sarge, they forced it on me.
WILSON	Well, give it back at once.
WALKER	All right, Sarge. Do you want a stick?
WILSON	No, thank you.

(THERE IS NOW SILENCE EXCEPT FOR EVERYONE SUCKING ROCK)

PIKE	It's gone all soft and sugary. I like it when it's like that, don't you, Joe?
WALKER	Yeh, smashing. It goes like that when it's been kept a long time; 1939 was a vintage year for rock.
WILSON	I can't wait any longer for Capt. Mainwaring, we've been here nearly two hours, we shall just have to carry out the battle plan without him. Pike, Walker, get your things together, we're going to establish a second command post at Godfrey's cottage. Pte. Sponge, you'll be in charge. Wait for half an hour then send out a patrol to report to me at Godfrey's cottage. Got that?
PRIVATE	Yes, Sarge.
PIKE	Can I bring my stick of rock with me, Uncle Arthur?
WILSON	No, you can't. Put it away. (HE OPENS THE SHOP DOOR) Come on.

FADE.

SCENE 7.
GODFREY'S COTTAGE. DUSK

MAIN AND FRAZER ARE PEERING OVER THE LEWIS GUN OUT OF THE FRONT WINDOW AND JONES AND GODFREY ARE PEERING OUT THE BACK. DOLLY AND CISSY ARE BOTH KNITTING. THE FURNITURE IS PILED AGAINST THE DOORS AND WINDOWS IN A STATE OF SIEGE.

FRAZER	(PEERING OUT) I don't like it, Captain Mainwaring, it's too quiet.
MAIN	Neither do I, Frazer. Can you see anything?
FRAZER	Not a thing, it will be dark soon.
MAIN	I wonder where the rest of the platoon are.
FRAZER	They probably had to leave the coach and make their way back on foot, as you know all civilian vehicles have to be put out of action during an invasion alarm.
MAIN	In that case, they wont be back for hours. (THERE IS A TERRIBLE SQUAWK FROM PERCY) Can't you keep that parrot quiet, Miss Godfrey?
DOLLY	(COMING OVER TO MAIN) Yes, he is rather sweet, isn't he. He belonged to our father, you know. He's nearly a hundred years old, the parrot, not our father – he died at ninety-two, five years ago. During the last year of his life, he was confined to his bed,

so we bought him the parrot to keep him company and it was during that time that he taught Percy to speak. Percy, say here comes the vicar, let's say our prayers.

PERCY   Take off your knickers, get up them stairs.

DOLLY   There you see, he was a very religious man, our father.

PERCY   You're not having a penny of my money, you old faggots.

DOLLY   I'm afraid our dear father never left us any money; he left it all to a young girl in the village. We could never understand why.

PERCY   A lovely bit of crumpet.

DOLLY   No, you're not having anything else, Percy. You've had your tea.

MAIN   Oh, for goodness sake cover that bird up, Frazer.

FRAZER   Ai, sir. (HE PUTS A CLOTH OVER THE CAGE)

JONES   (COMING OVER TO MAIN) Permission to speak, sir.

MAIN   What is it, Jones?

JONES   Can I go outside, sir?

MAIN   What? Oh yes, wait a minute, I'll come to the door and cover you. (THEY BOTH CROSS TO THE DOOR. MAIN OPENS IT) Off you go, Jones. (HE COVERS THE DOOR WITH HIS RIFLE)

FADE.

SCENE 8.
THE REVOLVING SUMMER HOUSE AT THE BOTTOM OF GODFREY'S GARDEN.

IT IS NOW DARK. WILSON, PIKE AND WALKER COME ROUND THE EDGE OF THE SUMMER HOUSE.

WILSON   It doesn't look to me as if there's anyone at home.

WALKER   Godfrey's two sisters are probably in bed, Sarge.

PIKE   Shall I nip round the front and look under the flower pot for the key.

WILSON   No wait a minute, I don't like the look of this, it's too quiet. (THERE IS A SOUND OF A FLUSH) What was that?

WALKER   Sounded like the what's name.

PIKE   (POINTING) Uncle Arthur, look, it's a German soldier coming out, look at his helmet.

WALKER   Blimey, he's right.

WILSON   Quick, take aim, fire!

(THREE SHOTS RING OUT)

CUT TO

SCENE 9.
INSIDE COTTAGE.

JONES STAGGERS THROUGH THE DOOR.

FRAZER   (DRAGGING JONES THROUGH THE DOOR) Quick inside, Jones. Shut the door. They're here, keep down, everyone.

(JONES IS TREMBLING WITH RAGE AND FIXING HIS BAYONET)

MAIN   What are you doing, Jones?

JONES   Heathen swine, I'm going to sort 'em out.

MAIN   Get down on the floor at once. Frazer, bring that Lewis gun over here.

FRAZER   Right, sir. Give me a hand, Jones.

(FRAZER AND JONES BRING THE LEWIS GUN OVER TO THE REAR WINDOW)

DOLLY   What was that noise, dear?

CISSY   I don't like to interrupt them, but we shall really have to ask them to draw the blinds and put the lights on. I can't see to knit.

FRAZER   All ready, sir, shall I fire?

MAIN   Wait a minute. Where did those shots come from, Godfrey?

GODFREY   From the direction of the revolving summer house, sir.

JONES   What's it do, Mr Godfrey?

GODFREY   Well, you see, you can turn it in whatever direction the sun's shining.

MAIN   Oh, shut up, Godfrey, have you got range, Frazer?

FRAZER   Ai, sir.

CUT TO

SCENE 10.
SUMMER HOUSE.

WALKER   Did you get him, Sarge?

WILSON   I don't know. We'd better take cover in here.

(ALL THREE CROUCH DOWN IN THE SUMMER HOUSE)

CUT TO

SCENE 11.
COTTAGE.

FRAZER WITH LEWIS GUN READY TO FIRE.

MAIN   Fire!

CUT TO

SCENE 12.
SUMMER HOUSE.

AS THE BULLETS HIT IT, IT STARTS TO REVOLVE.

CUT TO

SCENE 13.
COTTAGE.

WILSON   All right, hold your fire, Frazer.

DOLLY   We'd better get these tea things cleared away. You take the tray out to the kitchen, I think

Private Walker scrounges a cup of tea from the catering unit whilst filming on location.

there's enough light to see. I'd better not disturb them. I'll shake the cloth out of the window upstairs.

CUT TO

SCENE 14.
SUMMER HOUSE.

WALKER   (PEERING ROUND THE EDGE) 'Ere, Sarge, the cottage has disappeared.

WILSON   We're facing the wrong way, help me push this thing round.

(USING THEIR RIFLE BUTTS AS PADDLES, THEY PUSH THE SUMMER HOUSE ROUND)

PIKE   What do you think we ought to do now, Uncle Arthur?

WILSON   Oh, do stop calling me Uncle, Pike.

WALKER   'Ere, look at that, they're waving a great white cloth out of the window, they're surrendering. You'd better go in and accept it, Sarge.

WILSON   No, you go, Walker, I better stay here and keep an eye on things.

WALKER   Perhaps young Pike ought to go.

PIKE   Well, you're the oldest, Uncle, I mean Sergeant.

CUT TO

SCENE 15.
COTTAGE.

FRAZER   Mr Mainwaring, sir, they're surrendering, three of them are coming out with hankychiefs tied to their rifles.

MAIN   Well done, men, we showed them, eh! They might be up to their tricks, I'll make them come right into the room. Keep 'em covered, Frazer. (SHOUTING) Come in ze here. Put the lights on so we can get a good look at them. (JONES PUTS THE LIGHTS ON AND STANDS TREMBLING WITH HIS BAYONET. THE DOOR OPENS.) All right, come in ze here with your hands up. (WILSON, WALKER AND PIKE COME IN) Good heavens. Wilson.

WILSON   Mr Mainwaring.

MAIN
WILSON   (TOGETHER) You might have killed us.

(THE A.R.P. WARDEN BURSTS INTO THE ROOM)

WARDEN   Who's in charge here? Oh, I might have guessed. I'm going to get you good and proper this time. Light streaming all over the road, what's the idea, eh? Good job I was passing on my way home.

MAIN   What are you going home for, there's an invasion on?

WARDEN   What are you talking about?

MAIN   The church bells, of course.

WARDEN   That was a false alarm, we've been stood down for ages. Right, I'm going to book you all for flagrant disregard of blackout regulations. What do you say to that, eh?

PERCY   Take off your knickers, get up them stairs.

FADE.

DAD'S ARMY NO. 9

The Loneliness of the Long Distance Walker

CAST

Capt. George Mainwaring . . . . Arthur Lowe

Sgt. Arthur Wilson . . . . John Le Mesurier

L/Cpl. Jack Jones . . . . Clive Dunn

Pte. James Frazer . . . . John Laurie

Pte. Joe Walker . . . . James Beck

Pte. Charles Godfrey . . . . Arnold Ridley

Pte. Frank Pike . . . . Ian Lavender

Brigadier (War Office) . . . . Anthony Sharp

Chairwoman . . . . Diana King

Brigadier . . . . Patrick Waddington

Mr Reed . . . . Edward Evans

Capt. Cutts . . . . Michael Knowles

Blonde . . . . Gilda Perry

Soldier . . . . Larry Martin

Medical Officer . . . . Robert Lankesheer

Pte. Sponge . . . . .Colin Bean

Remainder of Platoon . . . . .Richard Jacques
Frank Godfrey
Alec Coleman
Hugh Cecil
Jimmy Mac
Desmond Callum-Jones
Vic Taylor
David Seaforth
Richard Kitteridge

Squeezing The Budget

Again in this programme we had to make great modifications and compromises in the settings that we were able to stage. The 'small room at the war office' was indeed very small and as I recall had to be pre-set in the church hall, which had to accommodate all the extra sets this week. This was not too inhibiting for the air-raid shelter, but it was a bit heartbreaking to be unable to devote the necessary space to the underground station which was so much a part of wartime London and a scene we would have loved to stage fully. We would also have liked to have found room for a substantial specially built courtroom-type set for the Hardships Tribunal scene, but space would not allow it and the budget forbade more location filming. We therefore compromised by making the tribunal use the church hall.

However, we splashed out a bit on the army medical centre. For this Harold Snoad, my assistant, found a wonderful location at the Regent's Park barracks. This was a glorious old Victorian edifice, still preserved and unspoiled. The persuasive Harold Snoad managed to obtain the necessary permissions and we were able to have a wonderful day's atmospheric filming.

By way of compensation we were able to afford some ace players for the other characters. The brigadier in the 'small room in the war office' was played by Anthony Sharp. He was an incomparable farceur whom I had first encountered while assisting on *Steptoe and Son* and unbeatable in the sorts of scenes where two slightly vague people get at cross-purposes with each other. His Captain Cutts was played by Michael Knowles, who was well known to Jimmy. He played the same sort of silly-ass captain in the other episodes of *Dad's Army* and was of course the captain in *It Ain't Half Hot Mum* and Teddy in *You Rang Milord?*

Diana King, who played Captain Peacock's wife for me in *Are You Being Served*, played the Lady Chairman. She was a very well-known actress even then and we were very lucky to get her. Edward Evans gave us an excellent Welshman as Mr Rees, and Larry Martin, who made other appearances in *Dad's* as a scruffy squaddie or an even scruffier Italian POW, played the greedy soldier. He later played Mr Mash for me in several series of *Are You Being Served*.

Patrick Waddington played the other brigadier from area command. Patrick was a well-known actor, mostly in musicals. In the twenties and thirties he had toured in a musical called *Prudence*, which starred my mother. He had also played the lead in many British films of the period. The profession had not been too kind to him in the sixties so I offered him, and he was pleased to accept, this very small part. Unfortunately all we could offer him by way of a set was a wobbly six-foot-wide flat and a very small desk. To cap this, when in rehearsal he picked up the telephone, it was covered in a thick layer of dust which he blew off, disdainfully muttering, 'Disgraceful!' John Laurie was standing at the side of the set. He rolled his eyes, and in a loud stage whisper hissed, 'The famous film star is having a temperament. Oh how the mighty have fallen.'

David Croft

SCENES

1.	CHURCH HALL
2.	SMALL ROOM IN THE WAR OFFICE
3.	AIR-RAID SHELTER
4.	UNDERGROUND STATION
5.	MAINWAIRING'S OFFICE AT BANK
6.	CHURCH HALL. DAY
7.	CHURCH HALL. LATE AT NIGHT
8.	FILM. BACK OF MEDICAL CENTRE
9.	CHURCH HALL
10.	CHURCH HALL OFFICE
11-14.	TELECINE
15.	WALKER IN UNDERWEAR
16.	TABLE IN MESS HALL
17-23.	TELECINE
24.	WALKER'S BUNK
25.	CHURCH HALL

SCENE 1.
CHURCH HALL.

WILSON   Private Godfrey?

GODFREY   Here, Sergeant.

WILSON   Platoon, attennn...shun. (HE SALUTES MAINWARING) Platoon ready for inspection, sir, bar one.

MAIN   Wilson – you're supposed to give me a piece of military information, not calling the odds. Who's missing?

WILSON   Private Walker, sir.

MAIN   He's bringing me a bottle of whisky tonight. I hope he's all right.

WILSON   So do I, sir. He's bringing me some cigarettes.

MAIN   (DRAWING WILSON TO ONE SIDE) Do you think we ought to send someone to his house to find out if anything's wrong?

(A MURMUR RUNS THROUGH THE PLATOON)

FRAZER   I don't like the look of this. I ordered a bottle of whisky.

JONES   He promised me a bottle of gin.

GODFREY   He's bringing me a box of fudge.

WILSON   Shall we carry on without him, sir?

MAIN   Yes, of course. Platoooooon – open order – march!

(THE DOOR BURSTS OPEN – WALKER RUSHES IN IN A TERRIBLE STATE. HE

'Reserved occupations' were jobs essential to the war effort. Sometimes they only applied to those over a certain age. Key railwaymen, electric- and gas- supply personnel and munitions workers were all reserved over that age. Coal mining took priority in this category. Coal was so vital that later in the war when men were called up they were given the choice of going into the forces or becoming a miner. They were called 'the Bevin Boys', after Ernest Bevin who thought of the idea.

STAGGERS UP TO MAINWARING AND SALUTES)

WALKER   I'm sorry I'm late, but I've got to go, you know.

MAIN   We all realise that, Walker. Fall in.

WALKER   No, sir. You don't understand. I've got to go. It's the medical.

MAIN   Well, you probably took too much of it. Are you all right now?

WALKER   No, sir. It's my call up! I've go to go for my medical in ten days' time.

MAIN   But I thought you were in the reserved occupation? What do you describe yourself as?

WALKER   I put myself down as a banana salesman and a wholesale supplier of illuminated signs. D'you think that's where I slipped up?

MAIN   This is serious news. You'd better fall the men out, Sergeant.

WILSON   Er, yes. Fall out, you chaps.

(THE MEN FALL OUT AND CROWD ROUND)

FRAZER   This is terrible news, Joe, terrible! What about my whisky?

JONES   And my gin?

GODFREY   What about my fudge?

MAIN   Don't be selfish, men. You're only thinking about yourselves. (TO WALKER) By the way, what about my whisky?

WALKER   I've got it in my bag, sir.

(HE OPENS HIS BAG, TAKES OUT A BOTTLE OF WHISKY FOR MAINWARING)

MAIN   Oh, that's good. Thank you. The point is, we really need you in the platoon. I mean, you're more important to us here than you would be there, eh, Wilson?

(WALKER HANDS WILSON HIS CIGARETTES)

WILSON   Definitely more important, sir.

MAIN   But you can't expect a lot of brass hats in Whitehall to know what the situation is. I mean, to them, Walker is just one of millions – an insignificant, nondescript nonentity.

(WALKER RESENTS THIS)

   But to us he's an important counterstone in our organisation. Well, this is a time for action, not words – don't you agree, Wilson?

WILSON   I always think it a good idea to keep the words down to an absolute minimum, sir.

MAIN   Precisely. We'll send a signal to the War Office pointing out that they've made a mistake

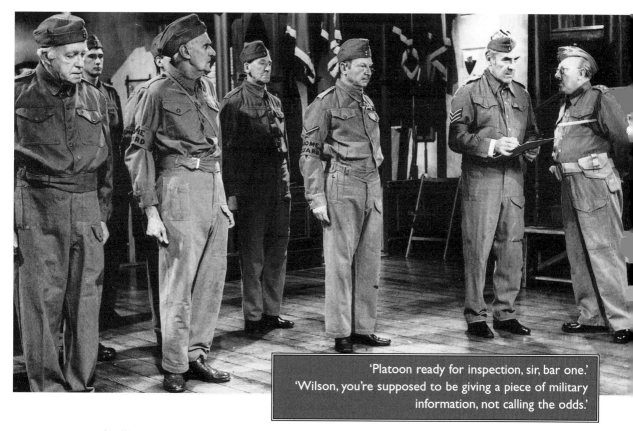

'Platoon ready for inspection, sir, bar one.'
'Wilson, you're supposed to be giving a piece of military information, not calling the odds.'

and telling them that we're jolly well coming to sort it out for them. You'd better phone it through, Wilson.

WILSON   I'm afraid we can't do that, sir. They won't take any more outgoing calls until we pay the bill.

MAIN   Oh, they haven't started that again, have they? Well, we'd better send a telegram. Take it down.

WILSON   I'll just go and get a pencil and paper, sir.

(WILSON GOES TO THE OFFICE)

JONES   Look, sir – I know a few dodges that will stop him from passing his medical. The best one is to drop some water in his ear 'oles. Plug 'em up with cotton wool and that'll make him deaf just long enough not to pass his medical.

MAIN   Jones! Are you suggesting that I should stoop to underhand tricks to stop Walker being called up?

JONES   No, sir – but it's the only way you'll do it.

MAIN   Nonsense! I shall tell them straight that he's more important to us than he would be in the army.

(WILSON RETURNS)

Now take this down, Wilson – 'To the Officer in Charge, Home Guard, War Office, Whitehall, London. Message begins – Desirable Walker not called up yet – Will call on you tomorrow – 5.00 p.m.' That should do the trick! 'Signed – Captain Mainwaring, Warmington-on-Sea Home Guard.'

WILSON   That'll cost 3/6d, sir – who's going to pay?

JONES   (HANDING HIM THE MONEY) Here you are, Mr Mainwaring – have this on me.

MAIN   Thank you, Jones. You'll see, men, as soon as they realise that I need him here, they'll call off this call-up. All right, Sergeant – carry on with the parade.

(CUT TO TELECINE SHOT – WAR OFFICE DURING WARTIME)

CUT TO

> Thirty years ago, if we wanted to show the exterior of a building to set up a location in a TV series, we simply stuck a still photograph on a music stand and took a close up. It may sound crude by today's standards, but in black and white it worked very well.

SCENE 2.
SMALL ROOM IN THE WAR OFFICE.

THE BRIGADIER IS SITTING BEHIND A DESK. HE IS A SCHOLASTIC 'JOE GRIMOND' TYPE. ON THE DESK ARE SEVERAL PHONES AND THREE SIGNAL LIGHTS – ONE OF THEM IS FLASHING.

BRIG.   (ON THE PHONE) I don't give a damn – I want it seen to at once, d'you understand – you're not the only one who's been up all night. I haven't left this desk for twenty-four hours. Now get on with it.

(HE SLAMS THE PHONE DOWN AS THE STAFF CAPTAIN ENTERS)

These armchair officers get on my nerves!

CAPT.   There's Mr Mainwaring and a Mr Wilson to see you, sir. They have an appointment for five o'clock.

BRIG.   Oh Lord! I'd forgotten all about them! It's that damned brother-in-law of mine, he's C.O. of this P.T. outfit and he's a mad-keen heel and toe merchant.

CAPT.   Heel and toe merchant, sir?

BRIG.   Long-distance walker. He won the London to Brighton race in '37. He wants to get together a crowd of fellows to make up a crack team.

CAPT.   What's this got to do with the Home Guard, sir?

BRIG.   Well, he thought that there'd be lots of fellows in the Home Guard units waiting for their call-up, so he asked me to send out a round robin to various units asking if they'd got any champions due to go into the army, and then I was to send him a list of the names and he'd try and get them transferred to his mob.

CAPT.   Did you have any luck?

BRIG.   No good at all – didn't get a single answer. That was until a few days ago – then I got this.

'I put myself down as a banana salesman and a wholesale supplier of illuminated signs. Do you think that's where I slipped up?'

(HE HANDS TELEGRAM PAPER TO THE CAPTAIN)

CAPT.   (READS) Desirable Walker not called up yet. Will call on you tomorrow – 5.00 p.m. Captain Mainwaring, First Platoon, Walmington-on-Sea Home Guard.

BRIG.   The odd thing is – that's not one of the units I sent a round robin to. Anyhow, I'll see them and get rid of them as quickly as possible. You'd think that stupid brother-in-law of mine would have more important things on his mind at a time like this. Still, the wife won't give me any peace until I do something about it, so let 'em in.

(CAPTAIN CROSSES TO THE DOOR AND OPENS IT)

CAPT.   Come in, please.

(MAIN AND WILSON ENTER)

BRIG.   Sit down, gentlemen. I can give you five minutes only. I'll just take down the details. What's this walker's name?

MAIN   I beg your pardon, sir?

BRIG.   The walker's name, man!

MAIN   Walker, sir.

BRIG.   I know that – I want his name.

WILSON   His name's Walker, sir.

BRIG.   Do you mean to say you've got a walker named Walker?

MAIN   Yes, sir.

BRIG.   That's unusual – eh, Cutts!

CAPT.   Oh, I don't know, sir. I knew a butcher named Butcher once.

BRIG.   Yes, perhaps you're right. Well – go on – what's his record?

MAIN   His record, sir?

BRIG.   He's got a record, hasn't he?

MAIN   (ASIDE TO WILSON) Has he got a record, Wilson?

WILSON   I don't think he's ever been found out, sir.

MAIN   No record, sir.

BRIG.   Well – is he good?

MAIN   Yes – very good, sir.

BRIG.   How the hell can he be good if he hasn't got a record?

MAIN   I don't think I follow you.

BRIG.   Look – is he one of the London to Brighton walkers?

MAIN   No, sir. I think he's one of the Warmington-on-Sea Walkers.

BRIG.   Sea walkers?

MAIN   No, J. Walker, sir.

BRIG.   Jay-walker!

MAIN   Yes, Joe Walker – that's his full name.

BRIG.   I know what his name is, but how d'you know he's a walker?

MAIN   Because he told us so!

WILSON   That's right – he said – 'I'm a Walker'.

BRIG.   Surely he said – not A. Walker – he said 'I'm J. Walker'.

> At the time we thought this sounded like a music hall routine but it worked remarkably well. We liked to think our later comedy had a bit more depth.

(THERE IS A PAUSE – THE BRIG. CLEARS HIS THROAT)

BRIG.   When is he due for call-up?

MAIN   Very soon. He goes for his medical next week.

BRIG.   Very well – leave it to me. I'll see what I can do. Good day.

MAIN   Thank you very much, sir.

(MAIN AND WILSON START TO GO. ONE OF THE LIGHTS ON THE DESK STARTS TO FLASH)

CAPT. (TO WILSON AND MAIN) That's the yellow warning – air-raid. You two had better go to the shelter in the basement. It's along the passage and down the stairs. Just follow the others. It's clearly marked.

MAIN   Oh, thanks. Er ... Good day.

(THEY BOTH GO)

BRIG.   A. Walker – J. Walker – those two are up the pole if you ask me. (TEARS UP THE PAPER) If my brother-in-law wants any walkers, he's just got to get them himself.

CAPT.   Hadn't we better beat it down to the shelters, sir?

> BRIG.   What! With those two lunatics? You can go if you like – I'd rather take my chances up here.

FADE.

'Wilson, take that man's name.'

SCENE 3.
AN AIR RAID SHELTER.

MAINWARING AND WILSON ARE SITTING SIDE BY SIDE ON A BENCH. THERE'S A
BRICK-WALL BACKING.

MAIN   (LOOKING AT WATCH) Just look at the time, Wilson! It's 7.30 p.m. – we've missed
our last train back. Well, we shall just have to wait for the all clear and then find a hotel
for the night.

WILSON   What about opening the bank in the morning, sir?

MAIN   They'll just have to wait until we get there, that's all. You don't seem to realise that
there's a war on, Wilson.

WILSON   No, sir.

MAIN   I must say it goes against the grain, Wilson, to be sitting here in this funk hole – while
our lads are tearing into them up there.

WILSON   If you become a casualty, sir, you'd only add to the burden of ...

MAIN (INTERRUPTING) ... an already overworked Civil Defence Organization. I know, Wilson, I know. It doesn't alter the fact that I want to be 'up and 'at em – the swines!

WILSON I think you'd better leave it to the spitfires, sir. That pistol in your pocket wouldn't do much harm to a Dornier at ten thousand feet.

MAIN I know that, Wilson.

WILSON After all, it didn't do much harm to that man-sized target at ten paces.

MAIN It's a very difficult weapon, Wilson. (SHUFFLING) Damned knobbly, too!

(THE ALL CLEAR SIREN SOUNDS)

MAIN Ah – there you go – come on, Wilson – we've got to find ourselves a hotel.

FADE.

SCENE 4.
UNDERGROUND STATION.

CLOSE UP OF MAINWARING'S HEAD ON PILLOW. BESIDE HIM IS A PRETTY BLONDE. ON THE OTHER SIDE IS WILSON'S HEAD.

MAIN Are you asleep, Wilson?

WILSON Not yet, sir.

BLONDE Are you sure you wouldn't like your friend to come and lie next to you?

WILSON No, thank you, madam. I'm quite comfortable where I am.

MAIN Jolly decent of you to make room like this – Miss – er?

BLONDE Just call me Judy.

MAIN Er ... well, my name's Mainwaring, and this is Mr Wilson.

WILSON How d'you do.

MAIN Well, good night – er, Judy. Goodnight, Wilson.

WILSON Good night, sir. Good night, Judy.

BLONDE Good night, boys.

(THE CAMERA PANS UP THE WALL AND WE SEE AN UNDERGROUND SIGN WHICH SAYS 'TRAFALGAR SQUARE'. WE PAN ALONG A ROW OF SLEEPING FIGURES.)

FADE.

SCENE 5.
MAINWARING'S OFFICE AT THE BANK.

THE OFFICE IS EMPTY. WE HEAR VOICES – THE DOOR OPENS, MAINWARING AND WILSON COME IN. THEY BOTH LOOK PRETTY SCRUFFY AND COULD DO WITH A SHAVE. PIKE FOLLOWS THEM IN.

MAIN   Oh, Pike – I want you to apologise to the staff for me. Tell them we were caught in an air raid and we had to wait for the first train back in the morning.

PIKE   Nasty thing to happen, sir.

(PIKE PICKS A LONG BLONDE HAIR FROM MAINWARING'S SHOULDER. MAINWARING HANGS UP HIS HAT, PUTS HIS HAND IN HIS OVERCOAT POCKET – PULLS OUT A SILK STOCKING. PIKE STARES AT IT. MAINWARING QUICKLY STUFFS IT BACK IN HIS POCKET)

MAIN   You see ... we ... er had to sleep in the underground. Things got a bit mixed up.

PIKE   Yes, sir! Was there anything else, sir?

MAIN   Of course there wasn't. Oh – I see what you mean. No thank you, Pike.

(PIKE GOES)

WILSON   Bit embarrassing, sir – the staff having to wait on the doorstep for us to open up the bank.

MAIN   Yes – as I was putting the key in the door, I distinctly heard that cheeky new girl humming 'Who Were You With Last Night?'

WILSON   Surely that was 'Run Rabbit Run', sir?

MAIN   You always were tone deaf, Wilson.

WILSON   If you don't mind me saying so, sir, you seem a bit edgy this morning.

MAIN   Edgy? Who wouldn't be edgy after a night in the underground?

WILSON   Didn't you sleep, sir?

MAIN   No, I did not! You know how important the hours before midnight are – as the trains didn't stop running until then, it was a bit difficult to doze off.

WILSON   I managed all right, sir.

MAIN   No doubt you did. But I happen to be a little bit more sensitive. I do not find that someone shouting 'Mind the doors, pass right down the car, let 'em off first, please' in my ear conducive to a good night's sleep.

WILSON   Well, I'll just pop off home to shave and change, sir. I haven't got much time – the committee is meeting at 11.30 a.m.

MAIN   Of course, I forgot – it's Wednesday. How much longer are you going to serve on that damned committee, Wilson?

WILSON   Only another three weeks, sir.

MAIN   Well, I'm glad to hear it, we're short-staffed enough as it is without having you miking off every Wednesday.

(HE SITS AT HIS DESK AND STARTS WORKING ON SOME PAPERS)

WILSON   I'm not miking off – as you so picturesquely put it. I was chosen – as a citizen of substance to – perform this really rather important public service.

MAIN   What precisely do you do – inspect the drains?

WILSON   It's the Military Service Hardship Committee, sir.

MAIN   Oh – pensions and boring stuff like that.

WILSON   No, it's for people with one-man businesses, who'll be ruined if they're called up.

MAIN   Oh, I see. Draft dodgers.

WILSON   Not all of them, sir. Some of them are quite genuine cases.

MAIN   Well, I'm sure that ... wait a minute ... Walker! He's got a one-man business.

WILSON   But if he's called up, he'll hardly be ruined.

MAIN   No – but we shall be.

WILSON   Ah – I'm sorry, sir, but I couldn't be a party to anything like that.

MAIN   I'm not suggesting anything underhand, Wilson. There's nothing to stop him going before the committee, is there?

WILSON   No, I suppose not, sir.

MAIN   And you'd be there to make sure he got a favourable hearing.

WILSON   I must emphasise, sir, that I shall have to be absolutely impartial.

MAIN   I shall expect you to be, Wilson. I shall expect you to be, and I know I can rely on you to banish from your mind the thought that if Walker goes, so will the cigarettes and the whisky. You will decide the case solely in the light of the mortal blow dealt to his struggling one-man business and the threat to the security of this island if we lose one of the only able-bodied men in our unit.

WILSON   But he will be in the army, sir.

MAIN   This is the place where Jerry is going to attack, Wilson – not Catterick. Well, it's obviously too late for him to go today, so he'll have to go next week. That's two days before his medical.

WILSON   There's quite a long waiting list, sir.

MAIN   There you go again, with your red-tape mentality. What does he have to do?

WILSON   He fills in an application form.

MAIN   Well, bring one back with you. We'll get it filled in tonight.

WILSON   Then he must have someone to speak for him. But not a lawyer or a solicitor. Just a reliable citizen of some repute.

MAIN   What could be better than a bank manager? Especially one of my standing. That settles it.

SCENE 6.
THE CHURCH HALL. DAY.

THE THREE MEMBERS OF THE COMMITTEE ARE SITTING AT A TABLE. THE CHAIRMAN IS A J.P. – A TIGHT-LIPPED EFFICIENT LOOKING LADY. THE TRADE UNION REPRESENTATIVE IS A STROPPY WELSHMAN – THE THIRD MEMBER OF THE PANEL IS WILSON. MAINWARING IS ADDRESSING THE TRIBUNAL. WALKER SITS BESIDE HIM.

MAIN   And in conclusion, may I urge the tribunal, with respect of course, but may I urge the tribunal to consider this is not a war in which gallant knights ride out to cross swords with the king's enemies – this is mortal combat – to the death – for every man whose veins course with English blood – every man Jack of us can throw out our chest and say – 'I'm a frontline solider'.

CHAIR   Not only the men, Mr Mainwaring!

MAIN   Precisely, er – Mrs Chairman – er Mrs Chairwoman. That is the point I am trying to make. Every man Jack and er ... and every woman Jack ... can throw out our ... well, you know the sort of thing I mean. And that Mr er ... Madam Chairman - woman – and er ... er ... gentlemen, is my case, on behalf of Joseph Walker.

(THERE IS A PAUSE. THE THREE MEMBERS OF THE TRIBUNAL PUT THEIR HEADS TOGETHER, WHISPER VIGOROUSLY)

CHAIR   Before we continue, I'm sure we'd like to thank Mr Mainwaring for coming here and assisting us. Do you second that, Mr Wilson?

WILSON   Oh yes – indeed I do. Mr Mainwaring has put Walker's case most ably. (LOOKING AT HIS WATCH) If at some length.

CHAIR   Do you wish to say something before we go any further, Mr Rees?

MR REES   Yes, Madam Chairwoman. Through the chair, I would like to say that we have heard a very eloquent speech from Mr Mainwaring, but none of it was really to the point. What we are here today to decide is if Mr Walker is called up, would it ruin his business – that and nothing else. The fact that Mr Mainwaring has extolled the virtues of Mr Walker has no bearing whatsoever on the case.

CHAIR   Thank you, Mr Rees. Have you anything else to add to that, Mr Wilson?

WILSON   I'm sure Mr Mainwaring is the last person in the world to waste the time of the tribunal deliberately – I think it was just ignorance of our procedure that led him to go – er – a little longer than was perhaps absolutely necessary.

CHAIR   Well, let's just get the details right. The address of your business, Mr Walker, is 1B, Slope Alley, just off High Street? You know, I've lived in Warmington-on-Sea all my life and I still can't place where your business is.

MR REES   Yes – through the chair, I'd like Mr Walker to tell us where his business is.

WALKER   (HOPING TO MAKE A GOOD IMPRESSION) Well, through the chair, I'll tell you.

CHAIR   No, no, Mr Walker – you don't go through the chair.

WALKER   Eh?

CHAIR   Mr Rees and Mr Wilson speak through the chair, but you speak to me.

WALKER   Oh!

CHAIR   You see, I am the chair! The chairman, Mr Walker.

WALKER   Oh – yeah – well, you go down the High Street just past Mr Mainwaring's bank – and carry on for about a hundred yards and Slope Alley is on your right. You go down it about twenty yards and you come to a little green door – you go through that and you'll find yourself in a yard.

CHAIR   And that's where your business is?

WALKER   No, not quite – that's where Sid Newman's business is – second-hand motor-car accessories – well you go through his yard – down at the bottom are a couple of old garages – that's where I am.

CHAIR   And how long has your business been established?

WALKER   Oh – about a year. I started just after the war broke out, as soon as I realised that things were going to er ... be in short ... (MAINWARING KICKS HIM) I mean, I was a bit short of money when I started it.

CHAIR   Mr Rees, have you any questions?

MR REES   Yes – I see you describe yourself as a wholesale supplier – what exactly does that mean?

'Do try and show a little enthusiasm, Wilson.'

'Poor fellow, he has no mother or father.'

WALKER	Well – it means that if you want something – I can get it for you.
MR REES	Be specific.
WALKER	(ASIDE TO MR MAINWARING) What's he mean?
MAIN	Tell him what you supply.
WALKER	Oh I see. Well – it all depends what you want.
CHAIR	Haven't you got a relation – someone who could run the business for the duration?
WALKER	No, I'm an orphan.
MAIN	Poor fellow – he has no mother – or father.
CHAIR	We know what an orphan is, Mr Mainwaring.
MAIN	I was not, for a second, suggesting otherwise.
WILSON	I am sure Mr Mainwaring has no intention of casting any slur on the intelligence of the tribunal – it's just that when one talks as much as Mr Mainwaring does – by the law of

averages – a certain amount of what he says is bound to be rather unnecessary.

CHAIR   Have you any questions, Mr Wilson?

WILSON   No, no.

(THE COMMITTEE PUT THEIR HEADS TOGETHER)

CHAIR   Well, before we come to a decision about your case, we'll have to see your books.

WALKER   (IN PANIC) Eh!

CHAIR   Your account books, have you brought them with you?

WALKER   No – I didn't think you'd want to see them.

CHAIR   Until you produce your books, Mr Walker, we cannot proceed with your case. Is this the last appeal today, Mr Wilson?

(WILSON NODS)

CHAIR   Then I'll be off – I'm late enough as it is.

(SHE GATHERS UP HER THINGS AND SWEEPS OUT)

MR REES   (GETTING UP AND CROSSING TO WALKER – ALL CHARM) Oh, by the way, boyo, let me have your card, will you? Might be able to do a little business before you're called up.

WALKER   (HANDING HIM CARD) Here you are, mate.

MR REES   Thanks. (HE GOES)

MAIN   I think we did very well, Walker. I think they were impressed with your case.

WALKER   Do you, sir?

MAIN   Well, of course, they'd be the last people in the world to allow their feelings to show.

WALKER   I got the impression they thought we were a couple of right Charlies!

MAIN   Well, I'm a pretty old hand at this game and, let me assure you, you're quite wrong. All we have to do is bring your books along next week and everything will be all right.

WALKER   I can't do that, Mr Mainwaring.

MAIN   Why not?

WALKER   I don't keep 'em.

MAIN   D'you mean to say you run a business and you don't keep books? I've never heard anything like it.

(WILSON COMES OVER)

MAIN   Ah – Wilson! Walker was just congratulating me on my handling of the case – though I must say you weren't much help, Wilson.

WILSON   Well, I told you, sir, I had to be impartial.

WALKER   Couldn't we cook up a set of books between us, Mr Mainwaring? After all you're a bank manager: you should know how.

MAIN   How dare you suggest such a thing, Walker. In all my years in banking, I have never heard anything so outrageous, I wash my hands of the whole affair. Good day.

WALKER   (APPEALING TO WILSON) What did I say?

FADE.

SCENE 7.
CHURCH HALL. LATE AT NIGHT.

JONES, PIKE, FRAZER, GODFREY AND WALKER ARE GROUPED TOGETHER. IN THE PICTURE IS A STEPLADDER AND A TIN BATH.

JONES   There's only one way out of this, Joe, we shall just have to make sure that you don't pass that medical tomorrow.

PIKE   I don't think Mr Mainwaring and Mr Wilson would approve of this, Mr Jones, it's not honest.

JONES   It may not be honest, son, but there are times in life when you just have to do something that's just a little bit naughty. Anyhow, it's for the good of the whole platoon. Come and give us a hand with this ladder.

(HE AND PIKE PULL THE LADDER INTO POSITION)

All right, Joe, get your shoes and socks off.

WALKER   What for?

JONES   You ain't got flat feet, have you?

WALKER   Course I ain't.

JONES   Well, you soon will have, all you've got to do is keep jumping off this ladder and remember to land flat-footed.

WALKER   I'm not doing that, it will hurt me.

JONES   Only at first, you'll soon get used to it.

FRAZER   Och! There's nothing to it, laddie.

(HE TAKES HIS SHOES AND SOCKS OFF)

As a Scot, I shall just have to set an example to you English as usual.

(HE STARTS TO CLIMB STEPS)

JONES   I shouldn't go too high, if I were you.

FRAZER   What do you mean?

JONES   Well, it's best to start at the bottom and work up.

FRAZER   Nonsense, we haven't got time.

JONES   Don't forget to land flat-footed.

FRAZER   (HE IS ABOUT FIVE STEPS UP)

I don't know, lot of fuss about nothing.

(HE JUMPS. CLOSE-UP OF HIS FACE ALL THE TIME. HE LANDS WITH A JARRING THUD. HIS FACE IS CONVULSED WITH AGONY. HE HAS A TERRIFIC STRUGGLE AS HE TRIES TO HIDE THE PAIN. HE SLOWLY PICKS UP HIS SHOES AND SOCKS AND HOBBLES TOWARD THE OFFICE. HE OPENS THE DOOR AND GOES IN. SUDDENLY FROM BEHIND THE CLOSED DOOR COMES A TERRIBLE HOWL OF AGONY THEN SILENCE)

WALKER   I'm sorry, but I'm not doing that.

JONES   Look, if you start from the bottom step and you hold on to someone's hand when you jump, you won't feel a thing. Hold his hand, Godfrey.

(GODFREY COYLY TAKES WALKER'S HAND)

Not now, when he's jumping. Come on, Joe, get on with it. (TO PIKE) You start counting, son.

(WALKER STARTS AT THE BOTTOM RUNG AND JUMPS OFF. EVERY TIME HE DOES HE GIVES A LITTLE 'OW'. PIKE COUNTS ONE)

FADE.

(WALKER IS STILL JUMPING AND HAS REACHES THE THIRD STEP. GODFREY IS STILL HOLDING HIS HAND)

PIKE	496.
WALKER	(JUMPING) Ow.
PIKE	497
WALKER	(JUMPS) Ow.
PIKE	498
WALKER	(JUMPS) Ow, that's the lot, I'm not doing any more.

(JONES PULLS TIN BATH INTO POSITION)

JONES   All right, stick your feet in here. (WALKER STEPS IN BATH) Now step on this newspaper. (WALKER STEPS ON PAPER) Now let's see the result. (WALKER STEPS OFF) (CLOSE-UP OF FOOTPRINTS) There you are, as flat as a pancake.

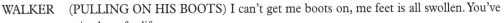

'...497..'

WALKER   (PULLING ON HIS BOOTS) I can't get me boots on, me feet is all swollen. You've ruined me for life.

JONES   Don't worry, lad, your feet will be as right as rain in a couple of days, just so long as they stay like that for the medical tomorrow, that's all you've got to worry about.

(DURING THIS GODFREY HAS CREPT UP BEHIND WALKER AND HE SUDDENLY BURSTS A PAPER BAG BEHIND HIS EAR. WALKER DOES NOT TURN A HAIR, BUT JONES JUMPS IN THE AIR)

JONES   What are you playing at?

GODFREY   I was trying to give him a fright.

JONES   What on earth for?

GODFREY   Turn his hair white, I thought it might make him look older.

JONES   Gimme strength. Now let me see, you was in the last lot, Jock, can you remember anything else you did at your medical.

FRAZER   I had to give a little cough.

JONES   Show us.

FRAZER   Ahem.

JONES   Was that all.

FRAZER	Yes.
JONES	There must have been something else.
FRAZER	I can't remember, it was a long time ago.
JONES	I can't either, we'll skip that for the minute. Now pay attention, this is the plan tomorrow. What time have you got to be at the medical board?
WALKER	9.30 a.m.
JONES	Right, you will leave your place at nine o'clock sharp, young Pike will come with you. You will run right round the town until you reach the medical centre at 9.20 a.m., keep running all the time. We shall be waiting for you round the back. By the time you get before that medical board, you'll be fit for ... fit for nothing.

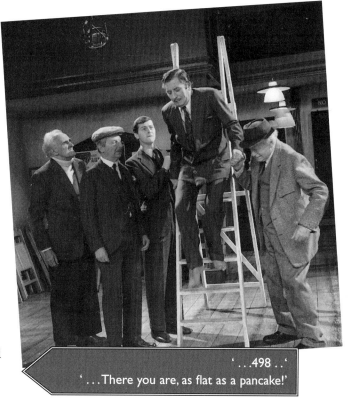

'...498..'
'...There you are, as flat as a pancake!'

FADE.

SCENE 8.
FILM. BACK OF MEDICAL CENTRE.
JONES, FRAZER AND GODFREY ARE STANDING IN A GROUP WAITING.

| JONES | Now the whole thing depends on split-second timing. (LOOKING AT WATCH) It's 9.20, and here he comes. |

(WALKER COMES INTO THE PICTURE WITH PIKE)

WALKER	(HE IS SO OUT OF BREATH HE CAN HARDLY SPEAK) Blimey, I'm all in, let me sit down.
JONES	You're not sitting down there, keep running. (WALKER RUNS ON THE SPOT) 'Ere, eat this. (HE HANDS HIM A LITTLE BIT OF SOAP)
WALKER	What's it for?
JONES	Makes the heart beat faster.

(HE DROPS IT IN WALKER'S MOUTH)

| WALKER | If my heart beats much faster, I'll take off. |

(WALKER HAS STARTED TO FOAM AT THE MOUTH)

'...Jock, can you remember anything else you did at your medical?'
'I had to give a little cough...'

JONES	All right, stand still a minute. (HE BLINDFOLDS HIM)
WALKER	What's this for?
JONES	It will put your eyes out of focus. I'll take it off at the last minute. Don't stop, keep running, keep going. (HE LOOKS AT HIS WATCH) 9.27. Right, start spinning him round.

(THEY SPIN HIM ROUND)

All right, mate, this is it, come on.

(JONES GETS HOLD OF WALKER'S HAND AND RUSHES HIM UP TO THE DOOR. HE WHIPS OFF THE BLINDFOLD AND PUSHES HIM THROUGH IT. THERE IS A LOUD

CRASH. THE OTHERS JOIN JONES ROUND THE DOOR)

JONES He'll be in there a good half-hour, we'd better wait and see what happens.

(WALKER STAGGERS OUT OF THE DOOR)

JONES Blimey, that was quick, did they turn you down?

WALKER No, they've cancelled it, it's not 'till tomorrow.

FADE.

SCENE 9.
CHURCH HALL H.Q.

THE MEN ARE DRAWN UP ON PARADE.

WILSON Parade at 6.30 tomorrow night. Platoon, attention. Dismiss.

(WALKER COMES OVER TO MAINWARING)

WALKER They passed me A.I. this afternoon, sir. That means I shall be leaving in about two weeks' time.

MAIN Well, I did my best for you, Walker, and I'm afraid we shall miss you, but duty's, duty.

(THE PHONE RINGS IN THE OFFICE)

Answer the phone, Wilson.

WILSON Yes, sir. (HE GOES INTO THE OFFICE)

WALKER I'd just like to say how much I appreciate all …

(WILSON RETURNS)

WILSON Excuse me, sir, it's for Walker, the brigadier at G.H.Q. wants to speak to him.

WALKER Blimey, I wonder what he wants.

(THEY ALL GO INTO THE OFFICE)

SCENE 10.
OFFICE.

WALKER PICKS UP PHONE.

WALKER Hullo, Private Walker 'ere.

(BRIGADIER ON PHONE. DIVIDED PICTURE)

BRIG. Look here, Walker, I was in Mr Mainwaring's office at the bank this afternoon and he gave me an excellent glass of whisky. I asked him how he managed to get it and he told me that you keep him supplied.

WALKER That's right, sir.

BRIG. Well, look here, can you let me have half a dozen bottles?

WALKER Yes, I think I can manage that, sir.

BRIG. Good man, let me have them as soon as possible, then you can make it a standing order for a half a dozen bottles every month.

WALKER I'm afraid I can't do that, sir.

BRIG.   Why not?

WALKER   I'm going into the army in two weeks' time, sir.

BRIG.   Oh are you, well don't worry, leave it to me, you're far more important to us here than you would be there. You can take it from me, you will not be called up.

WALKER   Do what, sir?

> It is worth noting that it was exceedingly hard to avoid military service during the war.

BRIG.   I said, you can take it from me, you will definitely not be called up.

(WALKER HANGS UP)

MAIN   What did he say, Walker?

WALKER   He said I can take it from him, I will definitely not be called up.

CUT TO.

SCENE 11.
TELECINE

SHOT OF BARRACK GATES. NOTICE 'INFANTRY TRAINING BARRACKS'. WALKER GOES THROUGH THEM WITH SMALL CASE. VOICES CAN BE HEARD SHOUTING COMMANDS. SOUNDS OF MEN MARCHING.

12. WALKER UNDER SHOWER.

13. SIDEBURNS BEING SHAVED OFF.

14. CLIPPER GIVING HIM A SHORT BACK AND SIDES.

15. WALKER STANDING IN HIS LONG WOOLLEN UNDERWEAR.

VOICE Battle dress trousers, two
(RUNNING ON THE SPOT)

Battle dress blouse, two.

Flannel shirts, two.

Woolen socks, four.

Greatcoat, one.

(MARCHING EFFECTS)

Boots, two etc. etc.

(EACH ITEM IS PLONKED INTO WALKER'S ARMS UNTIL HE IS LOADED DOWN)

SCENE 16

SECTION OF TABLE IN MESS HALL.

TWO PRIVATES ARE EATING. POSTER ON WALL: 'WE ARE NOT INTERESTED IN THE POSSIBILITIES OF DEFEAT. THEY DO NOT EXIST' QUEEN VICTORIA OR 'CARELESS TALK COSTS LIVES.' WALKER SITS BESIDE THEM WITH HIS MESS TIN FULL OF FOOD. THERE IS THE MOST TERRIBLE CLATTER. THE TWO OTHER MEN ARE LOOKING VERY GLUM.)

WALKER   (TO MAN) First army meal, eh!

MAN   What?

WALKER   I said, oh never mind.

(HE IS FED UP)

(HE STARTS TO EAT. HE PICKS UP CORNED-BEEF FRITTER ON HIS FORK)

What's this, then?

MAN   Eh?

WALKER   I said, what's this then?

(HE IS HOLDING HIS FRITTER ON HIS FORK)

MAN   Don't you want it? Ta!

(HE TAKES THE FRITTER OFF WALKER'S FORK AND PLONKS IT IN HIS OWN MESS TIN)

They're all right these corned-beef fritters.

(HE HAS HIS MOUTH STUFFED WITH FOOD AND HE SPLASHES WALKER AS HE TALKS. WALKER, FED UP, SLOWLY STARTS ON HIS REMAINING FRITTER)

WALKER   'Ere, this ain't bad, you know. It's a funny thing, but I've never tasted corned-beef before.

MAN   Eh!

WALKER   Oh, skip it.

(HE CHEWS THE REST OF THE FRITTER)

SCENE 17.

TELECINE

WALKER CLIMBS INTO HIS BUNK. BUGLE IN DISTANCE PLAYS LIGHTS OUT.

18. BARRACK ROOM WINDOWS LIGHTS GO OUT.

19. SHOT OF CLOCK ON TOWER AT TEN. THE LAST BUGLE NOTES FADE AWAY.

20. HANDS ON CLOCK MOVER ROUND TO TWO.

21. BARRACK ROOM WINDOWS. LIGHTS ALL GO ON.

22. FEET HURRYING ALONG PASSAGE. VOICE 'GET THE M.O. AT ONCE.'

23. KNOCKING. VOICE: 'COME AT ONCE, DOCTOR.' LOTS OF NOISE OF HURRYING FEET.

SCENE 24.
WALKER'S BUNK.

MEN ARE GATHERED ROUND WALKER'S BUNK. WE DO NOT SEE HIM. WE JUST HEAR HIS GROANS. VOICE 'LET THE DOCTOR THROUGH.' M.O. PUSHES HIS WAY THROUGH MEN.

M.O.　My God, what is it?

(CLOSE UP OF WALKER'S FACE. IT IS SWOLLEN AND HAD HUGE BLOTCHES ON IT. GROANS.)
FADE.

SCENE 25.
CHURCH HALL.
THE MEN ARE DRINKING TEA.

FRAZER　Go easy with that sugar, there's not much left.

PIKE　How are we going to get any more without Mr Walker?

JONES　I don't know, son, we're going to miss him, you know.

FRAZER　I still can't believe he's gone.

(DOORS BURST OPEN, WALKER ENTERS)

WALKER　All right, line up. I've got chocolate biscuits, hair grips and nylon.

(MAINWARING & WILSON COME OUT OF THE OFFICE)

MAIN　Good heavens, Walker, what are you doing here?

WALKER　I've got me ticket! I'm out!

MAIN　How?

WALKER　Simple, I'm allergic to corned-beef!!

(THE PLATOON ALL GATHER ROUND HIM SHAKING HIS HAND AND LAUGHING)
FADE.

'I've got me ticket! I'm out!'

DAD'S ARMY NO. 10

Sgt. Wilson's Little Secret

CAST

Capt. George Mainwaring	Arthur Lowe
Sgt. Arthur Wilson	John Le Mesurier
L/Cpl. Jack Jones	Clive Dunn
Pte. James Frazer	John Laurie
Pte. Joe Walker	James Beck
Pte. Charles Godfrey	Arnold Ridley
Pte. Frank Pike	Ian Lavender
Mrs Pike	Janet Davis
Little Arthur	Graham Harboard
Pte. Sponge	Colin Bean
Remainder of Platoon	Richard Jacques
	Frank Godfrey
	Alec Coleman
	Hugh Cecil
	Jimmy Mac
	Desmond Callum-Jones
	Vic Taylor
	David Seaforth
	Richard Kitteridge

Line-Up For Laughs

In this episode we did one of our 'line-up' scenes. Captain Mainwaring walks down the front of the platoon to inspect the various attempts by members of the squad to camouflage themselves. Remember this was episode 10 and we went on to write another 70. It was during this second series that Michael Mills, who was then head of Comedy at the BBC, said to us, 'Now look here, I don't think you should do any more of those "line-up" scenes.' Now Michael Mills had been a Lieutenant Commander in the navy during the war and was inclined to issue instructions in a similar way to a captain on a sailing ship, bawling out orders on the quarter deck during a force-ten gale. 'Don't do any more,' he shouted in the bar of the BBC Club one evening, 'the viewers will get bored with Arthur walking up and down inspecting the platoon. There's a limit to the amount of laughs you can get with the same joke, you know!' Well, we took no notice and went on to do dozens of 'line-ups' which never failed to get laughs. Not only that but we did them in *It Ain't Half Hot Mum* and even in *Hi De Hi*.

Michael Mills was an amazing person, a BBC man to his fingertips. He had tremendous enthusiasm, drive and energy, and his opinions were completely black and white. He either loved something or loathed it.

Fortunately, he loved *Dad's Army* right from the start, even when it was called *The Fighting Tigers*. In fact, as most people know, Michael thought up the title *Dad's Army*. He was a wonderful champion of the show and fought tooth and nail to get the series made. Michael was one of the great heads of comedy at the BBC. He was not given to procrastination: his motto was 'Get on with it!' He made snap decisions. If he liked the script he would call the writer into his office, look at a large planning map on the wall and say, 'Right, we'll make the pilot on such and such a date. I've already told Them Upstairs [referring, of course, to the other heads of department].'

It is difficult for people nowadays to understand what the BBC was like thirty years ago. In spite of still suffering from some of the snobbish and elitist attitudes of Reithian days, huge changes were taking place. Swift decisions were made and there was an enormous confidence in the air. Within a year all programmes would be in colour (this script was, of course, recorded in black and white), and a bunch of Oxbridge graduates would have started a series called *Monty Python's Flying Circus*. Michael Mills was a king amongst kings along with Hew Weldon, Tom Sloane, Bill Cotton, Paul Fox and David Attenborough, who would come and sit with us in the canteen and casually remark, 'What are you chaps going to do next?' We'd tell him and with complete trust he would say, 'Good luck with it.' It certainly was the golden age of TV.

Jimmy Perry

SCENES

1. CHURCH HALL

2. CHURCH HALL (LATER)

3. SIDE OFFICE (CHURCH HALL)

4. MRS PIKE'S SITTING ROOM

5. CHURCH HALL

6. SIDE OFFICE

7. MRS PIKE'S FRONT DOOR (NIGHT)

8. CHURCH HALL

SCENE 1.
CHURCH HALL.

THE PLATOON ARE DRAWN UP ON PARADE. WILSON IS IN CHARGE.

WILSON Now, before we fall out, I've been asked to draw your attention to an item in last week's newspaper which states that a member of the H.G. in the Midlands was fined £5.00 for being drunk in charge of his rifle.

JONES Permission to speak, Mr Wilson.

WILSON Yes, Jones.

JONES I'm sure you don't think any members of this platoon would behave like that, Mr Wilson. I think it's a bit of an insult to our integrity.

(CHORUS OF 'YES IT IS' ETC.)

WILSON I'm sure no offense was intended. Mr Mainwaring just asked me to draw your attention so that we might all benefit from the lesson.

FRAZER What lesson?

WALKER Don't take your gun to a party.

FRAZER Well, all I've got to say is, if Mr Mainwaring intends to insult us, he should do it to our faces instead of asking other people to do it.

(CHORUS OF 'THAT'S RIGHT' ETC.)

WILSON I'm sure Mr Mainwaring had no intention of insulting you.

FRAZER Well, why isn't he here?

WILSON He is here.

> There were over three million rifles, tommy guns and sundry automatic weapons that were kept by members of the Home Guard in their homes. Young boys under the age of eighteen were not allowed to take home any ammunition.

FRAZER　　What's he doing - hiding?

WILSON　　Yes, he is in a way.

JONES　　I'm not suprised, after making out we were a load of drunks.

PIKE　　Anyhow, my mum doesn't allow me to drink.

WALKER　　I mean, I don't mind a drink now and then, but, as Jonesy says, making out we're all a load of drunks, I think it's a bit of a liberty.

(THE WHOLE PLATOON ARE NOW THOROUGHLY UPSET)

WILSON　　Please, please calm down. Mr Mainwaring is going to give us a surprise lecture, so on the command, fall out, I want you to gather in a semicircle round the stage. Platoon, fall out.

(THE PLATOON FALL OUT AND GATHER ROUND THE STAGE MUTTERING)

WILSON　　(IN STAGE WHISPER) Are you ready, sir?

MAIN　　(FROM BEHIND CURTAIN) No, I'm not.

(THE CURTAINS SHAKE)

WILSON　　Hurry up, sir, the men are waiting.

MAIN　　Let them wait. I shall start when I'm ready and not before.

(PLATOON START SLOW HANDCLAP)

WILSON　　They're getting impatient, sir.

MAIN　　All right, Wilson, you can announce me.

WILSON　　Quiet please, now settle down. Capt. Mainwaring is now going to show us something unusual.

FRAZER　　What's he going to do, give us a comic turn?

WALKER　　What's unusual about that.

(MAINWARING COMES THROUGH THE CURTAIN, CAMOUFLAGE ALL OVER HIM. HE LOOKS LIKE A SMALL TREE)

MAIN　　Good evening, men. I expect you're all wondering why I'm dressed up like this.

FRAZER　　Aye, we are.

MAIN　　Now, men, seeing me like this, what do you think is going to be the subject of my lecture?

GODFREY　　Pruning fruit trees, sir.

MAIN　　No, Godfrey. Camouflage. Sgt. Wilson, draw back the curtains. (WILSON GOES UP ON THE STAGE) I shall also require your help, Jones. (JONES FOLLOWS HIM)

The obsession among the Home Guard was to fight as guerrillas and not to expose oneself to the enemy. This was the keynote of all training. 'Colonel Blimp' tactics of men advancing across open country were regarded with horror; a legacy from World War I when the casualties had been appalling.

'I wonder if I might be excused?' Godfrey's bladder was a constant source of amusement throughout the filming of the various series.

Now, men, camouflage is the art of merging with your background. (WILSON DRAWS CURTAINS) You observe how I stand against a plain background. All right, Jones, drop the backcloth with the woodland scene on it. (JONES DROPS IN A BACKCLOTH WITH A BANG. IT IS THE FIRESIDE SCENE FROM *CINDERELLA*. A HUGE MANTELPIECE, A HUGE BLAZING FIRE WITH A COAL SCUTTLE) You will observe how I blend in with the background. Now, can you suggest any way I can improve this camouflage?

WALKER   How about disguising yourself as a lump of coal, sir?

MAIN   What? (HE TURNS AND SEES THE CLOTH) Jones, you've let in the wrong backcloth.

JONES   What's that, sir?

MAIN   I want the 'woodland' scene.

JONES   What? Oh yes, sorry, sir.

(THERE IS A TERRIFIC CRASH AS JONES LETS IN A FRENCH FLAT. IT IS 'OUTSIDE THE PALACE GATES'. THERE IS A DOOR IN IT. THERE IS A HOWL OF AGONY FROM MAIN. THE FLAT HAS COME DOWN IN FRONT OF MAIN. ABOUT TWO INCHES IN FRONT OF HIS FACE.)

MAIN   (VOICE FROM BEHIND FLAT) That was my foot, Jones. What, what do you think you're doing? Jones! (THE DOOR IN THE FLAT OPENS AND MAIN COMES THROUGH) Jones, where are you? (HE WALKS INTO THE WINGS CALLING. THE DOOR OPENS AND JONES COMES THROUGH IT. HE CLOSES IT BEHIND HIM.)

JONES   (CALLING) Where are you, Mr Mainwaring?

(WILSON COMES ON TO CENTRE OF STAGE)

JONES   Where's Mr Mainwaring gone, Mr Wilson?

WILSON   He went round the back. (HE KNOCKS ON THE DOOR) Are you in there, sir?

MAIN   Of course I'm here. Open this door at once.

WILSON   (SHAKING THE DOOR) It seems to be stuck, sir. (TO JONES) Go round and help Mr Mainwaring to open the door. (JONES GOES INTO THE WINGS)

(THE DOOR BURSTS OPEN AND MAIN COMES THROUGH AND SLAMS IT BEHIND HIM)

MAIN   Get that woodland scene in, Wilson.

(WILSON GOES. THE DOOR RATTLES)

JONES   I can't get the door open, Mr Mainwaring.

(THE 'FRENCH FLAT' FLIES UP IN THE AIR. THERE IS NO SIGN OF JONES)

MAIN   Where are you, Jones?

JONES   (FROM 'FLIES') I'm up here, sir. I went up with it.

MAIN   Well, come down at once. Use the ladder at the side.

(MAIN IS NOW AT LAST STANDING IN FRONT OF THE 'WOODLAND' CLOTH)

MAIN   Now, men, what do you think of that?

WALKER   I think it's the best turn I've seen for a long time.

(THE PLATOON APPLAUD)

WILSON   (COMING ON FROM THE WINGS) Quiet, please.

MAIN   Thank you, Wilson. Now these are the points I want you to make a note of, men. (HE TAKES A SMALL BOOK OUT OF HIS POCKET) Now one of the first things we

Like Godfrey's waterworks, Frazer's catchphrase 'We're doomed!' became a regular feature of the show.

need are some corks. Champagne corks are the best. You cook them under the grill until they are burnt right through, and then ... (THUMBS THROUGH BOOK)

WALKER   You serve them on toast, very tasty, very sweet. (THEY ALL LAUGH)

WILSON   Quiet.

MAIN   (GLARING AT WALKER) You grind them to a powder, mix with grease and keep in an old tin. This mixture is applied to the face. Now, are there any questions so far?

FRAZER   Yes, how are we going to get hold of champagne corks, sir? Don't forget there's a war on.

MAIN   I'm well aware of that, Frazer. As usual we must improvise.

JONES   Permission to speak, sir.

MAIN   Yes, Jones.

JONES   What about getting a cork bath mat, sir, and cutting it into lumps?

MAIN   Excellent idea, Jones. Make a note of that, Wilson.

WALKER   You're going to have a job getting one of them, Mr Mainwaring, very scarce they are.

MAIN   Oh, really?

'Very tasty, very sweet' was a catch phrase of two wartime radio stars, Nan Kenway and Douglas Young, whose act consisted mostly of references to food.

WALKER   It so happens I've got one only left in stock. Seeing as it's for the platoon. 30/- right?

MAIN   Oh, very well. If you use it sparingly, one bath mat should be enough for the whole platoon. Now, working from head to toe, we start with the helmet. You will notice the grass tucked under the net is kept fairly short. This is so that it will blend in with most backgrounds. Now if I had tall tufts of grass sticking out of my helmet it would look a bit odd.

WALKER   Especially if you was trying to hide on a bowling green.

WILSON   Quiet.

MAIN   You will observe that the rest of me is covered in foliage. Now are there any questions?

FRAZER   Yes. What do you do in the winter when you can't get any foliage?

MAIN   That's a good question. Now has anyone got any ideas?

JONES   What about covering yourself in holly leaves, sir?

MAIN   An excellent idea, Jones, you just cover yourself in holly instead of foliage.

GODFREY   But supposing you're covered in holly leaves and you want to be excused?

MAIN   Well, you er ... just have to use your own initiative, Godfrey. So don't forget, men, your main task is to break up your outline. Now I want you to parade back here in one hour's time and I want everyone to camouflage themselves. Is that clear? (THERE IS A SOUND OF A DOG BARKING) What's that, Wilson?

WILSON   Sounds like a dog, sir.

MAIN   What, all right, platoon, dismiss.

(MAIN RUNS OFF STAGE)

FADE.

SCENE 2.
CHURCH HALL.

THE MEN ARE ALL DRAWN UP ON PARADE WITH VARIOUS FORMS OF
CAMOUFLAGE ON.

MAIN   Excellent turnout, men. Don't you think so, Wilson?

WILSON   Yes, absolutely first class, sir.

(MAIN STOPS IN FRONT OF THE FIRST MAN. HE IS COVERED FROM HEAD TO FOOT
IN HAY)

MAIN   (ASIDE TO WILSON) Who's this, Wilson?

WILSON   I haven't the faintest idea, sir.

(WALKER PULLS ASIDE THE HAY AND POKES HIS HEAD THROUGH)

WALKER   It's me, sir. I'm a small haystack.

MAIN   Good gracious, that's good, don't you think, Wilson?

WILSON   Awfully good, sir.

(SUDDENLY THERE IS A TERRIFIC SNEEZE FROM YOUNG PIKE WHO IS STANDING

BESIDE WALKER. HE SNEEZES AGAIN. HIS EYES ARE RUNNING AND HE IS IN A TERRIBLE STATE)

MAIN   What on earth's the matter with you, boy?

PIKE   I can't stand it, sir, it's my hayfever.

MAIN   Well don't stand next to him then; move to the end of the line.

PIKE   Yes, sir.

(HE MOVES TO THE END OF THE LINE. MAIN MOVES ON TO GODFREY WHO IS WEARING A BEE-KEEPERS MASK AND VEIL WHICH IS FULL OF HOLES. HE IS ALSO WEARING A LAY OF FLOWERS ROUND HIS NECK)

MAIN   What's this supposed to be, Godfrey?

GODFREY   Well, I tried several things on, sir, and none of them really seemed to suit me.

MAIN   But you're supposed to break up your outline.

GODFREY   I thought it looked pretty broken up as it is, sir.

MAIN   What's that you've got round your face?

GODFREY   It's my bee-keeping mask, sir.

MAIN   But it's full of holes.

GODFREY   It's all right, my bees are quite friendly.

MAIN   (TOUCHING THE 'LAY') But why this? It looks as if you're going on a cruise to the South Seas.

GODFREY   Well, I got the idea from a film I saw at the Odeon last week. It was called the *South of Pago Pago*. It had Dorothy Lamour and Victor Mature in it, it was awfully good.

MAIN   What's that got to do with camouflage?

GODFREY   I don't know really, sir, I just thought it looked rather er ... open air.

MAIN   I see (HE MOVES ON).

WILSON   He's right, you know, sir, it does look open air.

(MAIN GIVES HIM A GLANCE AND STOPS IN FRONT OF FRAZER, WHO HAS A BATTERED TOP HAT ON HIS HEAD AND A TATTY BIT OF WHITE SHEETING ROUND HIS SHOULDERS LIKE A CLOAK).

MAIN   What are you going as, Frazer? The Phantom of the Opera?

FRAZER   No, this is a winter camouflage, sir, you wear it in the snow.

(HE CROUCHES DOWN. TURNS THE SHEET SO THAT IT FALLS IN FRONT OF HIM. IT HAS THREE BLACK BUTTONS PAINTED ON IT. ON THE BACK OF HIS HEAD HE HAS A SNOWMAN MASK WHICH HE TURNS ROUND. HE REPLACES TOP HAT AND STICK WITH A PIPE IN HIS MOUTH.)

MAIN   Well done, Frazer (HE PASSES ON TO JONES WHO IS WEARING HIS BUTCHERS OUTFIT, STRAW HAT AND APRON) Why aren't you wearing camouflage, Jones?

JONES   I am, sir. I'm camouflaged as a butcher.

MAIN   I don't think I quite follow you.

JONES   Well, sir, I'm standing outside my shop, right. (MAIN NODS) A Jerry soldier comes along, he don't know I'm in the Home Guard, he thinks I'm a butcher, right. (MAIN NODS) Then when he's not looking, whop! Right up with the old cold steel. And that's one thing they don't like, you know, sir.

MAIN   Yes, thank you, Jones, I'm well aware of that fact.

(HE PASSES ON TO PIKE WHO IS WEARING HIS UNIFORM AND NO CAMOUFLAGE)

MAIN   What's the meaning of this, Pike?

PIKE   I've got a note for you, Mr Mainwaring, it's from my mum. (HE HANDS MAIN THE NOTE. MAIN TAKES IT AND MOVES DOWN WITH WILSON)

MAIN   (READS) 'I don't want young Frank covered in a lot of damp leaves, it will only set off his chest again.' Right, this is the finish, Wilson, I want to speak to you in my office as soon as parade's over.

FADE.

SCENE 3.
SIDE OFFICE.

MAIN IS SITTING AT HIS DESK.
WILSON IS STANDING.

MAIN   I've never heard anything like it in all my life, Wilson. The way Mrs Pike mollycoddles her son is absurd. Always sending notes and coming down here and interfering with the running of the platoon. I tell you, Wilson, it has to stop.

WILSON   Yes, sir.

'I've got a note from my mum ...' Pike's excuses were a constant irritation for Mainwaring.

MAIN   I mean, supposing all the other men arrived with notes from their mothers. It would look a bit odd, wouldn't it?

WILSON   It certainly would, sir, at their ages.

MAIN   The fact is, Wilson, someone has got to talk to Mrs Pike and, as you're quite friendly with her, I think it ought to be you. You are quite friendly with her, aren't you, Wilson?

WILSON   Well, I take her out to the cinema now and then.

MAIN   I see.

WILSON   I quite often go round and have a meal with her and that sort of thing.

MAIN   What sort of thing?

WILSON	Well, whatever she happens to be cooking at the time, sir.
MAIN	Oh.
WILSON	You see, she has my ration book and that makes things a lot easier.
MAIN	Yes, I'm sure it does. The point is you've got to tell her, Wilson. I mean, I wouldn't even allow my wife to tell me how to run this platoon. She knows that a woman's place is in the home.

(HE GETS UP FROM THE DESK AND CROSSES THE ROOM TO PUT SOME PAPERS IN A FILE)

And never for one moment would I tolerate her telling me what to do.

(THE PHONE RINGS)

WILSON	(PICKING UP THE PHONE) Hullo, yes … Oh, good evening, Mrs Mainwaring. It's your wife, sir.
MAIN	(TAKING THE PHONE) Hullo, Elizabeth … Yes … Look, I'm very busy just at the moment. I'm afraid I shan't be home for another half an hour. What's that? Yes, Elizabeth … yes, Elizabeth … Very well, dear. I'll come right away. (HE HANGS UP AND GIVES WILSON A SICKLY GRIN) The little woman, you know, Wilson. (HE GIVES A FALSE LAUGH) I'll leave you to lock up, and by the way, don't forget to talk to Mrs Pike. Put your foot down, Wilson. (HE GOES)
WILSON	Yes, sir, I'll do just that.

FADE.

SCENE 4.
MRS PIKE'S HOUSE.

THE SITTING ROOM. FRANK & MRS PIKE ARE HAVING TEA.
MRS PIKE IS READING A LETTER.

MRS PIKE	Oh, dear.
FRANK	What is it, Mum?
MRS PIKE	It's from the W.V.S. They want to know if we can take in one evacuee. I suppose we ought to do all we can to help. I think we could manage one all right. He can have that little room at the back. I'll write and let them know tonight.
FRANK	Isn't Uncle Arthur supposed to be coming to tea today, Mum?
MRS PIKE	I expect he'll be here in a minute. You don't mind do you?
FRANK	No, Mum, I quite like Uncle Arthur.
MRS PIKE	No. I mean you don't mind us having a little evacuee to stay with us.
FRANK	No, I don't mind.

(CUT TO OUTSIDE DOOR. WILSON IS JUST ABOUT TO COME INTO THE ROOM. THE DOOR IS SLIGHTLY OPEN)

MRS PIKE'S VOICE	The trouble is children growing up so quickly. Still, I must say it will be nice to have a little child about the house again.

97

(WILSON FREEZES OUTSIDE THE DOOR WITH HIS HAND ON THE KNOB)

FRANK'S
    VOICE   I wonder if it will be a boy or a girl?

MRS PIKE'S
    VOICE   We shall just have to wait and see won't we?

(CLOSE UP OF ARTHUR'S FACE, AGHAST)

    You know, Frank, it's going to be funny being a mother again after all these years. Oh, don't say anything to Uncle Arthur about this just at the moment, let me tell him in my own time.

FRANK'S
    VOICE   Sure, Mum.

(WILSON LOOKING VERY FAINT, PULLS HIMSELF TOGETHER, PUSHES THE DOOR OPEN AND ENTERS THE ROOM)

MRS PIKE   There you are, Arthur, you are late. Well, hurry up and sit down or the tea will get cold. You look very pale, are you all right?

WILSON   What ... er, yes.

MRS PIKE   He does look pale, doesn't he, Frank?

FRANK   You know what they say, Mum, pale and passionate. (HE LAUGHS)

MRS PIKE   Now that will do, Frank. Hurry up and finish your tea.

(SHE POURS OUT A CUP OF TEA FOR WILSON)

MRS PIKE   Don't you want anything to eat, Arthur?

WILSON   What ... no, not just now, thank you.

MRS PIKE   (OFFERING HIM A PLATE OF CAKES) Wouldn't you like one of my baby rock cakes?

WILSON   No thank you, Mavis.

MRS PIKE   Well, you must eat something. I know, I managed to get some of those nursery biscuits today. I'll fetch them. (SHE STARTS TO RISE)

WILSON   Please don't bother, Mavis. I'm quite all right.

MRS PIKE   But you like nursery biscuits, Arthur, they're your favourite. They've got icing on top with little children on them.

WILSON   I know perfectly well what they look like, Mavis, and I don't want any.

MRS PIKE   There's no need to snap like that, Arthur, especially after me using all my points to get them.

WILSON   I'm sorry, I'm just not hungry.

MRS PIKE   Well, if I had known I wouldn't have wasted my points on them. I've got to be very careful with everything on points, you know.

FRANK   It seems about the only thing you can have these days that's not on points is a baby.

MRS PIKE   Now, Frank, don't be coarse. I'm sure I don't know where you get it from, unless it's from some of these rough men in the Home Guard. I think I shall speak to Mr Mainwaring about it.

WILSON   Mavis, please.

FRANK   Well, I'd better get into my uniform, Mum, it will soon be time for parade.

(HE GETS UP AND GOES)

MRS PIKE   I don't know what's the matter with you tonight, Arthur. It's not like you to look so miserable all the time.

WILSON   Look, Mavis, I couldn't help overhearing what you was saying to Frank just now.

MRS PIKE   Oh, you mean the addition to the family.

WILSON   Er, yes.

MRS PIKE   Well, why should you worry about it?

WILSON   Of course I worry. I just can't understand why you're taking it so calmly, Mavis.

(SHE STARTS TO CLEAR AWAY THE TEA THINGS)

MRS PIKE   Well what do you expect me to do? I mean it isn't as if I'm the only woman in this situation.

WILSON   But I feel responsible, Mavis.

MRS PIKE   I don't see why you should. After all, I'm the

> one who decided to have the child.

WILSON   But why?

MRS PIKE   Why, because there's a war on and we must all do our bit.

WILSON   But what's the war got to do with it?

MRS PIKE   Well, I wouldn't be having the child if there wasn't a war on, would I?

(AS SHE IS MOVING ABOUT CLEARING THE TABLE, HE FOLLOWS HER ABOUT)

> Oh, Arthur, do stop trailing about after me like a lost sheep, I'm trying to get on. You'd better go now or you'll be late for parade.

WILSON   But, Mavis ...

(FRANK COMES IN IN HIS UNIFORM)

FRANK   Are you ready, Uncle Arthur ... (GLARE FROM WILSON) I mean Sgt?

FADE.

SCENE 5
CHURCH HALL.

THE PLATOON ARE SITTING ON BENCHES IN A HALF CIRCLE.
MAIN & WILSON ARE STANDING.

MAIN   As you know, men, in order to stimulate keenness, we are starting a competition each month for the best suggestions for improvised weapons of means of defence. A prize will be awarded for best idea which will be paid for out of platoon funds and supplied by L/Cpl. Jones. What have you got for us, Jones?

JONES   Half a pound of liver and two lamb chops, sir.

MAIN   Do you hear that, men? Half a pound of liver and two lamb chops, a worthy prize indeed. Now, we have three entries, Sgt. Wilson, Pte. Frazer and Pte. Walker. Sgt. Wilson will demonstrate his idea first. Sgt. Wilson.

(WILSON DOES NOT HEAR, HE IS MILES AWAY)

> Sgt. Wilson.

WILSON   Yes, sir?

MAIN   We're waiting for you to demonstrate your grenade firing crossbow.

WILSON   My what, sir?

MAIN   Your grenade firing crossbow.

WILSON   (WHISPERING) I'm terribly sorry, sir, I'm afraid I've left it at home.

MAIN   (DRAWING HIM TO ONE SIDE) What on earth's the matter with you, Wilson? You've been in a dream all the evening. You're not ill are you?

WILSON   No, sir.

MAIN   Well, just pull yourself together. I'll speak to you after parade. (HE COMES DOWN TO THE MEN AGAIN) Our next entry is Pte. Frazer who will demonstrate an anti-tank device.

(FRAZER STEPS FORWARD WITH A PILE OF WHITE DINNER PLATES)

FRAZER   Now, sir, this is the road, right. I place a row of dinner plates upside down in a line right across it, so. (HE LAYS THE PLATES ACROSS THE ROOM)

MAIN   You did say this was an anti-tank trap, Frazer?

FRAZER   Aye, sir. That's right.

MAIN   Dinner plates?

FRAZER   Yes, sir, dinner plates.

MAIN   Please continue.

FRAZER   (GIVING HIM A GLARE) Now, the enemy tank comes down the road. Suddenly he sees the row of plates lying in his path. He doesn't know what they are, so he stops and opens his turret and gets out to have a look. Meanwhile, we're hiding behind cover and as soon as he gets out of his tank we let him have it – ping. How's that, sir?

MAIN   Not bad at all, Frazer.

FRAZER   Thank you, sir.

MAIN   Our next entry is Pte. Walker.

> **This was true fact taken from a Home Guard training manual.**

(WALKER COMES INTO THE PICTURE WITH JONES WHO IS WEARING HALF AN OLD TYRE ROUND HIS SHOULDERS LIKE A YOLK.)

WALKER   Right, now I'd like to demonstrate me 'All purpose shoulder protector.' You'll observe that it's made from half an old rubber tyre. This will protect the shoulders from shrapnel or a blow from a weapon, so.
(HE DRAWS HIS BAYONET AND GIVES JONES A CUT ACROSS EACH SHOULDER)

JONES   Didn't feel a thing.

MAIN   Two excellent suggestions.

Now, I think we'll settle this in a democratic fashion by a show of hands. Now, hands up who liked Frazer's idea ...

(SIX HANDS GO UP)

... and Walker's idea.

(SEVEN HANDS GO UP)

Walker is the winner.

(FRAZER GIVES A BLACK LOOK AND MUTTERS)

WALKER   (TO FRAZER) Don't take it to heart, 'Taf.' I'll give you one of my lamb chops.

MAIN   There's no doubt that Walker's idea is first class. I think we ought to equip the whole platoon. Let me see, there's seventeen of us, that means we shall require nine old tyres.

WALKER   There's just one snag about this idea, Mr Mainwaring.

MAIN   What's that?

WALKER   It's very difficult to get old tyres, rubber's like gold in wartime.

MAIN   Well, what did you want to suggest it for in the first place? You'd better give Frazer the liver.

FRAZER   Aye. (HE GOES TO GRAB THE LIVER)

WALKER   'Old on a minute, I said they were difficult to get, I didn't say impossible.

MAIN   What do you mean?

WALKER   It so happens I've got a few old tyres in stock. I can let you have nine at 10/- each. How's that?

MAIN   It's outrageous! Besides, we only need eight and a half tyres.

WALKER   All right, I'll tell you what, I'll do you nine for four quid.

MAIN   Jones.

JONES   Yes, sir?

MAIN   Dismiss the men. (TO WILSON) Wilson, I want to see you in the office now.

WILSON   Oh, er .... yes, sir.

(MAIN CROSSES TO THE OFFICE FOLLOWED BY WILSON)

JONES   All right, fall in.

(CUT TO OFFICE)

> Very few of our scripts failed to mention food. Due to strict wartime rationing food became an obsession with the public, spawning jokes and songs on the radio like, 'When Can I Have A Banana Again' and articles in the newspapers. For all the shortages (very little meat, fats and sugar), the British people were never healthier than they were in the wartime years.

SCENE 6.
OFFICE.

MAIN ENTERS FOLLOWED BY WILSON. IN THE BACKGROUND WE CAN HEAR JONES DISMISSING THE MEN.

MAIN   Come in, Wilson and close the door.

Frazer gives a black look and mutters...

WILSON	Yes, sir. (HE CLOSES THE DOOR)
MAIN	Now, what's the matter, Wilson?
WILSON	Matter, sir?
MAIN	Yes, you've been in a day dream all night. Several times I've spoken to you and you haven't been listening and on top of that you go and leave your grenade firing crossbow behind.
WILSON	Well, sir. It's a bit difficult.
MAIN	You'd better sit down, Wilson.

(WILSON SITS)

	Now, what is it? Are you in some kind of trouble?
WILSON	It's not me that's in trouble, sir, it's er ... Mrs Pike.
MAIN	What do you mean, Wilson?
WILSON	(SHUFFLING HIS FEET) She's, er ... she's, er.
MAIN	Now look, Wilson, I'm not only your commanding officer, I'm also your friend and you need have no hesitation in confiding in me. Now, what's all this about Mrs Pike?
WILSON	(BLURTING IT OUT) She's going to have a baby, sir.

MAIN Oh good, I expect her husband will be delighted and ... but she's a widow, isn't she?

WILSON Yes.

MAIN Then how can she have a baby?

(THERE IS A SILENCE – THEY BOTH STARE AT EACH OTHER)

I thought you said you only went round there for meals!

WILSON Well, I told you she had my ration card, sir.

MAIN Yes and now she's got something else. I really can't believe my ears. I've come to the conclusion I don't know you, Wilson – you're a cad, that's what you are. How long have you known her?

WILSON Quite a number of years, sir.

MAIN   Then why on earth haven't you asked her to marry you?

WILSON   Well, sir, I've never really got round to it.

MAIN   Well, you'd better get round to it now. You can't go about behaving like Errol Flynn, you know. What do you think the Directors of the bank would say if they knew?

WILSON   I've really no idea, sir.

MAIN   Well, I have. There's only one thing for it, you must do the honorable decent thing and ask her to marry you.

WILSON   Yes, I think you're right, sir. I'll have a word with her in the next few days.

MAIN   You'll have a word with her tonight, Wilson. You don't seem to realise there's no time to lose.

WILSON   But it's Tuesday, sir.

MAIN   What on earth has that got to do with it?

WILSON   Well, she'll be in bed and asleep. She always goes to bed early on a Tuesday.

MAIN   How do you know ... I mean you'll just have to wake her up, and when I see you at the bank at nine o'clock

After he gets over the initial shock, the first thing Mainwaring thinks about is, 'What will people say?' A bank employee, or anyone from a big corporation could quite easily be dismissed for such behaviour in those days. Lord Reith, Head of the BBC, sacked a well-known radio producer because he was the innocent party in a divorce case.

The platoon did eventually form an honour guard, but not for Wilson and Mrs Pike. Jonesy's wedding to Mrs Fox was in the very last episode.

tomorrow morning I shall expect to hear that it's all settled.

WILSON   Very well, sir.

FADE.

SCENE 7.
THE FRONT DOOR OF MRS PIKE'S HOUSE.

WILSON COMES INTO THE PICTURE. HE GIVES A FURTIVE LOOK ROUND AND RINGS THE DOOR BELL. SILENCE. HE RINGS THE BELL AGAIN. THERE IS THE SOUND OF A WINDOW OPENING ABOVE HIS HEAD.

MRS PIKE'S

VOICE   Who's that?

WILSON   (STEPPING BACK AND LOOKING UP) It's me, Mavis. I must speak to you at once.

MRS PIKE   What on earth do you want at this time of night?

WILSON   It's only ten o'clock. I must see you at once.

MRS PIKE   Really, what will the neighbours think? All right, I'll come down. (SHE CLOSES THE WINDOW)

(THERE IS A DEADLY SILENCE. WILSON WAITS. SUDDENLY, A FIGURE COMES OUT OF THE DARKNESS. IT'S A POLICEMAN)

P.C.   May I see your identity card, sir?

WILSON   (TURNS, STARTLED) What?

P.C.   Oh, it's you, Mr Wilson, sorry. I saw a figure in the dark so I thought I'd better check up.

WILSON   Oh!

P.C.   On some sort of night exercise are you, sir?

WILSON   Yes, that's right.

P.C.   That's funny, I haven't seen any more of your chaps about.

WILSON   Well, I'm sort of on my own, you see.

(THE LETTERBOX OPENS AND MRS PIKE CALLS THROUGH)

MRS PIKE   Arthur darling, are you still there?

WILSON   (WITH A GLANCE AT P.C.) Yes, I'm still here, Mavis.

MRS PIKE   Good job you arrived when you did, I've only just got undressed.

(P.C. GIVES WILSON A LOOK. WILSON LOOKS DESPERATE)

MRS PIKE   Another five minutes and I should have been in bed and asleep.

WILSON   Mavis, please. (HE GIVES THE P.C. A DESPERATE LOOK)

P.C.   Well, I'll be pushing on then, Mr Wilson. It's rotten being up all night on duty, don't you think? Still, that's war. Good night, sir. (HE GOES)

WILSON   Why on earth don't you open the door, Mavis?

MRS PIKE   I can't. I've taken the blackout down. Besides, I've got my mother staying with me for a few days. What would she think?

WILSON   But I want to talk to you.

MRS PIKE   Well, you can talk through the letterbox.

WILSON   Oh really, this is absurd.

MRS PIKE   What is it you want to say?

WILSON   (HISSING THROUGH LETTERBOX) Will you marry me?

(THERE IS A SILENCE. SUDDENLY THERE IS THE SOUND OF A BOLT BEING DRAWN. THE DOOR FLIES OPEN AND MRS PIKE THROWS HERSELF IN WILSON'S ARMS. THE LIGHT FROM THE HALL FLOODS OUT)

MRS PIKE   Arthur, darling!

VOICE   Put that light out!

FADE.

SCENE 8.
CHURCH HALL.

THE MEN ARE DRAWN UP ON PARADE.

MAIN I'm dismissing you a little early tonight, men. As you know, Sgt. Wilson and Mrs Pike are getting married next Saturday and we are going to provide the guard of honour. Now, I want to have a little rehearsal, so we'll assume that the door at the back of the hall is the entrance to the church. Now, on command fall out, I want you to form two ranks each side of the door. Platoon, attention! Fall out.

(THEY DO SO, GET RID OF THEIR RIFLES AND FORM TWO RANKS EACH SIDE OF THE DOOR)

Now, when Mr and Mrs Wilson appear, I want you to draw your bayonets and form an arch, have you got that? (THEY ALL NOD) All right, Wilson, take your place by the door.

WILSON Oh, really, sir, is this necessary?

MAIN Of course it's necessary. We want to get it right, don't we? Go and take your place by the door. Wait a minute, we need someone to stand in for Mrs Pike. Now who's about her height?

JONES Can I volunteer for that, sir?

MAIN Good man, Jones. Go and stand on Sergeant Wilson's left. Right, now get into position.

(THEY DO SO. WILSON IS HATING EVERY MINUTE OF IT)

Right, are you ready? Now come through the doors. Take his arm, Jones. Guard of honour, present bayonets!

(THEY DO SO. WILSON AND JONES WALK SLOWLY BETWEEN THE RANKS)

For goodness sake, smile, Wilson. It's your wedding day!

(THE DOOR OPENS AND MRS PIKE RUSHES IN)

MRS PIKE (TO WILSON) Arthur, Arthur, our little friend's arrived.

WILSON My god!

MRS PIKE It's a dear little boy.

WILSON But that's impossible.

MRS PIKE And you'll never guess ... his name's Arthur, too. (SHE CALLS THROUGH THE DOOR) Come along, dear.

(A LITTLE BOY ABOUT TEN ENTERS)

(MRS PIKE TAKES HIS HAND AND LEADS HIM OVER TO WILSON)

BOY 'Ullo, are you my Uncle Arfer!

END.

> Difficult to imagine these days, but we actually received letters of complaint after this show went out, claiming it was immoral, lewd and a bad example to young people. Needless to say, Wilson never did get round to marrying Mrs Pike.

DAD'S ARMY NO. 11

A Stripe for Frazer

CAST

Capt. George Mainwaring ....Arthur Lowe

Sgt. Arthur Wilson ....John Le Mesurier

L/Cpl. Jack Jones ....Clive Dunn

Pte. James Frazer ....John Laurie

Pte. Joe Walker ....James Beck

Pte. Charles Godfrey...................................Arnold Ridley

Pte. Frank Pike ....Ian Lavender

Corporal-Colonel Square....................Geoffrey Lumsden

Capt. Bailey..John Ringham

Policeman...Gordon Peters

Caretaker ....Edward Sinclair

Pte. Sponge ....Colin Bean

Remainder of Platoon...........................Richard Jacques
Frank Godfrey
Alec Coleman
Hugh Cecil
Jimmy Mac
Desmond Callum-Jones
Vic Taylor
David Seaforth
Richard Kitteridge

The Show's Unluckiest Actors

This programme marks the reappearance of two of the unluckiest actors ever to be in *Dad's Army*.

First, John Ringham was cast as Mr Bracewell, the superior, dinerjacketed member of the first ever platoon of the Walmington-on-Sea Home Guard. He was the character who, when lined up on the first parade of the gallant band, had the temerity to say to Captain Mainwaring, 'Do you think you're going to be long?' To which he received the reply, 'Well that rather depends on Jerry, doesn't it?' He was going to a party for his wife's birthday and, of course, Walker sold him a black market wristwatch for a present. He was excellent in the part but after we had done the pilot, Jimmy and I came to the conclusion that the character was in many respects too similar to that of Godfrey, and the politeness and gentility of his character would be fulfilled by Godfrey. John appeared several times in the series as various officers, and was a most useful actor with a great sense of comedy.

Also, appearing as a policeman, was Gordon Peters. Gordon had played the part of the chief fire officer in the very first pilot episode of *Dad's*. In addition to the mayhem caused by the air-raid warden, we had written a hilarious scene where the chief fire officer had decided to hold a fire exercise in the church hall. He proceeded to fill it with fire hoses at the same time that Captain Mainwaring was

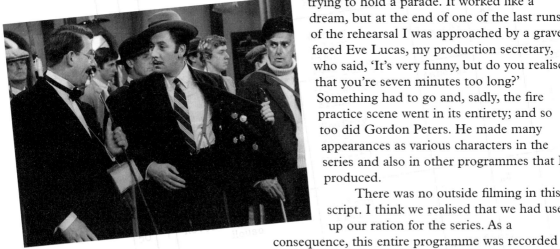

trying to hold a parade. It worked like a dream, but at the end of one of the last runs of the rehearsal I was approached by a gravefaced Eve Lucas, my production secretary, who said, 'It's very funny, but do you realise that you're seven minutes too long?' Something had to go and, sadly, the fire practice scene went in its entirety; and so too did Gordon Peters. He made many appearances as various characters in the series and also in other programmes that I produced.

There was no outside filming in this script. I think we realised that we had used up our ration for the series. As a consequence, this entire programme was recorded in the studio. There were four studios available of adequate size to record these programmes: studios three, four, six and eight. This particular series used each of them at one time or another. There was one very large studio - studio one - which we tried to avoid, as the cavernous nature of it made it pretty bad for comedy. The audience and the cast seemed to get lost in it and the reaction time of the laughter seemed to be delayed, something which the artists found off-putting.

David Croft

SCENES

1. THE CHURCH HALL
2. SIDE OFFICE
3. THE CHURCH HALL
4. SIDE OFFICE

SCENE 1.
THE CHURCH HALL.

THE PLATOON IS ASSEMBLED WITH UNIFORMS AND WITH RIFLES. WILSON IS
DRILLING THEM. MAINWARING IS IN THE SIDE OFFICE.

WILSON Platoon, 'Shun, stand at ease. I thought that the whole movement lacked nerve. Try and put a bit more sparkle into it. Platoon, 'Shun!

(JONES ENTERS)

JONES Sorry I'm late, Sarge.

WILSON Fall in, Corporal Jones. Try to be on time in future.

JONES I wouldn't have been late now, Sarge, but you see the offal comes in today and they haven't sent no suet.

WILSON Settle down. Platoon, for inspection port ...

JONES Hang on, I haven't got my bunduk.

WILSON Hurry up, Jones!

(JONES GOES TO THE CORNER TO GET HIS RIFLE)

> 'Bunduk' was a word for rifle frequently used by old soldiers. It comes from the Urdu.

JONES It's been one of those days today!

WILSON Yes, Jones, but we have to get on with the parade, you know, in spite of the absence of your suet.

(JONES RETURNS WITH HIS RIFLE)

JONES I promised it to Mrs Prosser of the WVS, you see, sir. (TO FRAZER) She was doing dumplings. She don't like the lads to go without their dumplings.

WILSON Be quiet, Jones! For inspection p--------ort arms! As you were. Now, your left hands are coming up to catch the rifle far too soon. You should whip the left hand up at the very last second. Try again. For inspection, p-----ort arms.

(GODFREY DOESN'T CATCH HIS RIFLE AND IT FALLS TO THE GROUND)

GODFREY I left it a bit late and er ... it wasn't there.

WILSON Pick it up. Now, let's try again. For inspection port--

(MAINWARING RUSHES IN WAVING A RATTLE AND WEARING HIS GAS MASK.
EVERYONE ELSE STANDS TRANSFIXED. MAINWARING CONTINUES WITH THE
RATTLE AND SHOUTING 'Gas, Gas ...' FROM INSIDE HIS MASK. SEEING NO
REACTION, HE TAKES OF THE MASK)

    MAIN   What are you all standing there for? You know what this is, don't you? It's a warning that the enemy is attacking with gas – now what are you all waiting for?

  FRAZER   We're still at attention! It's up to him at the end there to take his finger out!

(INDICATING WILSON)

    MAIN   Frazer! You will not use that sort of expression concerning my NCOs, either on or off parade. Is that understood?

  FRAZER   Yes, sir.

    MAIN   Good. At the same time, Wilson, I think it's up to you to take your ... to take some action.

  WILSON   Yes, sir. Right. (HE SHOUTS) Gas attack – Gas attack, on the command 'fall out', put on your gas masks. Fall o...ut.

(GENERAL CONFUSION AS THEY ALL TRY TO HANDLE THEIR RIFLES, HATS AND EQUIPMENT AND GET THEIR MASKS ON. WALKER DOES NOT MOVE)

    MAIN   Come on – you'll have to be quicker than that, you know. You're all choking by now. Walker, what's the matter with you? Get that flap open and the face piece on.

        (HE GOES UP TO WALKER AND STARTS TO OPEN THE FLAP)

        It's creeping into your lungs – you can't breathe. What's this?

(HE SEES SOMETHING INSIDE THE GAS MASK)

WALKER   Whisky, sir.

MAIN   Whisky! Do you realise you could be court-martialled for this?

WALKER   It's for Sergeant.

MAIN   Come over here.

(MAINWARING TAKES HIM TO ONE SIDE)

    Wilson!

(WILSON COMES BEHIND MAINWARING. HE'S WEARING HIS GAS MASK)

    Wilson, what have you got to say about this?

(HE TURNS AND SEES WILSON)

    Take that damned thing off!

(HE POINTS TO THE FOUR HALF-BOTTLES IN THE CASE)

    Now, is this yours?

WILSON   W-ell – yes, sort of.

MAIN   What kind of answer is that?

WILSON   Well, it's not all mine, sir. Only one bottle.

MAIN   I see. Who else is in this conspiracy?

(FRAZER, JONES AND GODFREY PUT UP THEIR HANDS. THEY ALL WEAR MASKS)

Although Godfrey could usually be relied upon to mess up a parade ground drill, it was Corporal Jones who eventually became the platoon's biggest liability in this department.

Jonesy launches into another tale of past glories.

MAIN	Take their names, Sergeant.
WILSON	That's rather difficult, sir – not being able to see their faces.
MAIN	I never knew a man like you for finding excuses.
WILSON	I suppose I could put little chalk crosses on them and take their names later.
MAIN	These are fighting troops, Sergeant, not Ali Baba and the forty thieves!
WILSON	Er, yes, sir. How would it be if you sounded the all clear?

(FIXING HIM WITH A STARE, MAINWARING BLOWS BLASTS ON HIS POLICE WHISTLE)

MAIN	Now come forward and collect this damned stuff.
JONES	How much was it, Joe?
WALKER	A pound a time, Jonesy.
JONES	(FEELING IN HIS POCKETS) Here we are then.
MAIN	We'll save the cash transactions until after the parade, Jones.

> In the original Arabian Nights story, crosses were put on the outside of the olive jars to indicate in which ones the thieves were hiding.

JONES   Yes, sir. Sorry, sir.

GODFREY   It's not for me – it's for my sister. Every time the sirens go, she has a funny turn.

MAIN   Back to your place, Godfrey.

(FRAZER IS GETTING HIS BOTTLE)

MAIN   Take their names, Sergeant.

WILSON   Jones, Godfrey, Frazer ...

FRAZER   Is there a regulation in the army that stops a Scotsman buying a bottle of whisky?

MAIN   Section forty – conduct to the prejudice of good order and military discipline. Back to your place, Frazer.

(INDICATING WALKER'S HAVERSACK)

    What's that at the bottom?

WALKER   (HOLDING UP BOX) Your cigars!

WILSON   (STILL WRITING) Mainwaring ...

MAIN   Now listen to me, you chaps, it's quite clear that your state of preparation against toxic gases is simply deplorable. Those masks must be on in a flash. As soon as you hear this. (HE WAVES THIS RATTLE) They must stay on until you hear this. (HE BLOWS THE WHISTLE AGAIN)

(ENTER POLICEMAN WITH TRUNCHEON DRAWN)

P.C.   What's the trouble?

MAIN   No trouble, Officer.

P.C.   Somebody was blowing for assistance.

MAIN   Aah! You mean this – it was for gas.

P.C.   Gas – blimey!

(HE STARTS TO PUT ON HIS GAS MASK)

MAIN   It's all right, Officer, just a practice alert.

P.C.   Oh, I see. Ah well, you can't be too careful these days, can you?

> This was the last episode that Mainwaring addressed the platoon as 'chaps'. We changed it to 'men'. We thought this was less democratic and more in keeping with Mainwaring's character.

MAIN   Just what I was telling my men.

P.C.   (ON THE WAY OUT HE TURNS) If you're doing anymore whistling, you might just tip me the wink first.

MAIN   Certainly, officer, certainly.

P.C.   Otherwise, when I hear that, I jump to it.

FRAZER   We're playing the East Littleton platoon on Saturday, so hands up for referee!

MAIN   That will do, Frazer! I want you all to practice getting into your masks in double quick time, so that if Hitler does blow this cowardly weapon on us, it will be no ball. Carry on, Corporal Jones.

'These hats are for officers only ...'

(MAINWARING GOES TOWARDS SIDE OFFICE WITH WILSON)

JONES   Yes, sir, of course, sir.

FRAZER   (ASIDE) If he bowls, it will be a no ball. What a lot of blather he comes out with.

JONES   That will be enough of that, Frazer. Now, on the command 'Go', I want you to shove your 'mushes' smartly in the face piece.

CUT TO

SCENE 2.
SIDE OFFICE.

MAINWARING AND WILSON ENTER.

WILSON   Do you want this list of names, sir?

MAIN   No, I think it would be best if we forgot about the whole episode. Have a word with Walker and tell him to stop using his respirator to carry all his contraband.

WILSON   Perhaps it would be a good idea if we issue him with one of those large Bren Gun

Ammunition pouches.

MAIN   Good idea. Go and get the Bren Gun, we can call him in.

(HE OPENS THE DRAWER OF HIS DESK AND TAKES OUT A HAT)

What d'you think of this, Wilson?

(IT'S A 'CHEESE CUTTER' TYPE OF OFFICER'S HAT. HE PUTS IT ON)

WILSON   Oh, I say, that's rather dinky.

MAIN   Suits me better than the forage cap, don't you think?

WILSON   Yes, sir. Your face doesn't look nearly so round and moonlike.

(MAINWARING REACTS)

WILSON   Oh yes, excellent. I think I'll get one.

MAIN   Oh no, you won't. These are for officers only.

WILSON   Ah, I might have guessed.

(HE TURNS AWAY)

MAIN   Anyway, it wouldn't suit you – the jaunting of the forage cap offsets that craggy, careworn face and polite undertaker manner of yours.

(THERE IS A KNOCK AT THE DOOR. ENTER JONES)

JONES   Permission to speak, sir.

MAIN   Yes, Jones.

JONES   They're getting much quicker, sir – and there's that bit of steak I promised you.

MAIN   (PUTTING IT AWAY QUICKLY) Thank you, Jones. Er, back to duty.

JONES   (AT DOOR) Permission to make a personal remark, sir!

MAIN   What is it, Jones?

JONES   That hat, it suits you a fair treat, sir!

(THERE IS ANOTHER KNOCK AT THE DOOR)

MAIN   Thank you, Corporal Jones. Come in …

(ENTER ARMY CAPTAIN – CAPTAIN BAILEY)

BAILEY   Captain Mainwaring?

MAIN   That's right.

BAILEY   Ah, I'm from Div. Ack. and Quack.

(THEY SALUTE. MAINWARING REMAINS SEATED)

MAIN   This is my Sergeant – Sergeant Wilson – Captain Ack. and Quack.

BAILEY   That's not my name. It stands for Assistant Adjutant Quartermaster General. I'm staff Captain A. Brought a few bits of bumf round and the new standing orders.

MAIN   Thank you very much.

BAILEY   Good news for you on the establishment side. You can make somebody up to a Corporal. That gives you a Sergeant, a Corporal and a Lance Corporal.

MAIN   That's good news, isn't it, Wilson?

This was one of the last times Godfrey was seen with a rifle. Eventually, in a later episode called 'Branded', we exchanged Godfrey's rifle for a first aid satchel with a red cross on it.

WILSON   I suppose it is.

MAIN   Well, of course it is. On Friday night when Jones is counting coupons, there's been no-one to give orders to.

BAILEY   Well, you can make them up as soon as you like. Just give the names to Adj.

MAIN   He'll have them this pip. We don't dally when it comes to decisions.

BAILEY   Good, I'll come along then.

(HE SALUTES, MAINWARING SALUTES BACK)

Oh, and don't let the old man catch you saluting sitting down. Drives him round the bend.

(MAINWARING STANDS UP APOLOGETICALLY)

MAIN   Oh, oh – does it? I'll remember.

(BAILEY TURNS AT THE DOOR)

BAILEY   He's a stickler about uniform too. So don't wear the hat with battledress- only with field service uniform.

MAIN   But I don't have a field service uniform.

BAILEY   In that case, don't wear that hat!

(BAILEY GOES)

MAIN   Damned red tape!

WILSON   (SURPRESSING A LAUGH) It's a pity, sir. Seemed to make you look more like an officer.

(MAINWARING REACTS)

WILSON   You go on wearing it, sir. I'll get one of the lads to keep cavey – when the old man appears you can do a quick switch.

MAIN   Never mind about that for now, we have the question of these promotions to consider.

WILSON   Yes, an extra Corporal. I suppose we give Jones another stripe.

MAIN   Well, of course, he has the maturity – there's no denying that – and the experience – and the guts.

WILSON   And the meat!

MAIN   Well, we have to disregard those sort of things and decide purely on the grounds of the national interest.

WILSON   Of course, I realise that – only it's my turn for rump next week.

MAIN   I think the wisest strategy would be to make up another Lance Corporal and see who shows the best potential. The question is who?

WILSON   I favour one of the younger men.

MAIN   Mrs Pike's boy for instance?

WILSON   Well, he is one of the younger ones.

MAIN   I didn't think you were speaking to the Pikes.

WILSON   Oh yes, I'm speaking to them, they're not speaking to me.

MAIN   What do you expect after leaving Mrs Pike stranded at the altar?

WILSON   I didn't leave her stranded, there were plenty of other people there.

MAIN   You can't expect me to give the boy a stripe because you didn't give his mother a wedding ring.

WILSON   I happen to think he'd make a good NCO.

MAIN   He'd be called up in no time and we'll be no further forward. We need someone who'll remain on the strength.

WILSON   Walker?

MAIN   No – he'd have access to the stores. Before we know where we are, he'd be flogging the

	bayonets for carving knives. We need a man of integrity.
WILSON	Godfrey? He's honest as the day is long.
MAIN	But could he lead men?
WILSON	Well, not from the front, he couldn't keep up.
MAIN	Then there's his bladder trouble.
WILSON	Well, at least we'd know where to find him.
MAIN	No, for my money, the man for the job is Frazer.
WILSON	I don't think he'd be right, sir. If there's any grumbling it always seems to come from him.
MAIN	It could be a case of the preacher turned game keeper. He was a Jack Tar, wasn't he?
WILSON	I believe so.
MAIN	One thing you can say for the boys in blue – they stand firm in the face of the enemy.
WILSON	Well, there's nowhere to run, is there?
MAIN	I pride myself I'm a good judge of character, Wilson. He's our man, mark my words. Call him in.
WILSON	Very good, sir. (HE GOES TO THE DOOR) Frazer!
FRAZER	What's up now?
WILSON	Would you mind coming into the office.
MAIN	It's an order, Wilson! (HE SHOUTS) Frazer! In here at the double!
FRAZER	(TO THE MAN NEXT TO HIM) Regimental bastard! (FRAZER CROSSES TO THE OFFICE AND AMBLES UP TO THE DESK AND SALUTES) Was there something you wanted?
MAIN	(RISES AND SALUTES) Yes, stand at ease, Frazer. We want a word with you. Sit down.

(FRAZER LOOKS AROUND)

FRAZER	What on?
MAIN	Where are the chairs, Wilson?
WILSON	The vicar took them, sir.
MAIN	He'd no damned right to.
WILSON	He needed some extra – for the young mother's club. It appears that since that Canadian unit moved into the district there are rather more girls in the club.
MAIN	Well stand easy, Frazer. Now Sergeant Wilson and I have been watching you very closely in the last few weeks.
FRAZER	Ay, well I'm sorry, but it's all this damned bull. I canna see the sense in it.
MAIN	Oh, come, come, Frazer – you can't say we spend hours blancoing our belts and gaiters in this unit.
FRAZER	That's only because we haven't got any belts and gaiters. We've all got a tin of blanc, tho' – ready for when they arrive.

'Jones, I want you to be the first to know that I'm making Frazer here up to Lance Corporal.'

MAIN   A smart soldier is a good soldier, Frazer, but I haven't called you in here to discuss spit and polish. We're looking for NCOs, and if I'm any judge of a man you have the necessary qualities of leadership, discipline and reliability. You held NCO rank in the navy, didn't you?

FRAZER   Ay, I did that. Chief Petty Officer – before I was busted.

MAIN   Busted?

FRAZER   Ay, I hit the officer of the watch.

MAIN   Did you?

FRAZER   With a boat hook.

MAIN   Oh dear!

FRAZER   The crooked end.

MAIN   Well, I'm sure you must have had a very good reason.

FRAZER   Oh, I had that.

MAIN   (TO WILSON) I thought so.

FRAZER   I was drunk.

MAIN   Well, that's all in the past. There's not much danger of that happening again, is there, Wilson?

WILSON   Not with a boat hook, sir.

MAIN   Do I take it you'll accept the stripe?

FRAZER   Ay, I will.

MAIN   Good man. Sergeant Wilson – get Jones.

WILSON   Yes, sir.

(HE OPENS THE DOOR. JONES, HAVING BEEN LISTENING AT THE KEYHOLE, FALLS IN)

JONES   Ah, just giving the brass handle a bit of a rub, sir.

WILSON   It's a china one!

JONES   Ah, that accounts for why it wouldn't take the shine.

MAIN   Jones, I want you to be the first to know that I'm making Frazer here up to Lance Corporal.

JONES   Permission to speak, sir.

MAIN   Yes, Jones.

JONES   A very good choice.

MAIN   We now have the establishment for a full Corporal.

JONES   That's good news, sir.

MAIN   It would be quite natural for you to think that your seniority would entitle you to that extra stripe.

JONES   Yes, sir.

MAIN   However, as the Commander in the field, I have to ensure that we get the right man with the best fighting potential.

JONES   I've got that all right. Just you let me get at 'em, sir. I'll be in the front there, with my cold steel. They don't like it up 'em!

MAIN   We will, therefore, select our Corporal from our two Lance Corporals.

JONES   Ah, a competition like. Well, that seems fair, don't it, Mr Frazer.

FRAZER   It will be if you stop bribing them with steak.

MAIN   I can assure you, Frazer, that Corporal Jones's activities as a tradesman have no influence whatsoever in our conclusions.

JONES   Ah. Well I wouldn't want to take any advantage or be prejudicious, Mr Mainwaring, sir. (TO FRAZER) I'll tell you what, I'll hold up their supplies until they've given the stripe.

FRAZER	Ay, I'd like that fine.
JONES	And when they've decided, they can have it again (TO MAIN) or not – as the case may be.
MAIN	Er – yes. Well, come with me, Frazer. We'll announce your promotion to the platoon.

(HE CROSSES TO THE DOOR)

FRAZER	Aye, aye, sir.
JONES	I've a couple of stripes at home you can have.
FRAZER	I'll buy my own, thank you very much.

(THEY BOTH GO)

JONES	Well, Sergeant Wilson, may the best man win.
WILSON	That's very sporting of you, Jonesey. Yes, indeed, may the best man win, though actually I'd prefer you to get it.

> We faded to black here and played
> 'Faithful Forever' from Gulliver's Travels.

FADE.

SCENE 3.
THE CHURCH HALL.

FADE UP TO THE MAIN CHURCH HALL. THE PLATOON IS DRAWN UP. FRAZER IS CAMERA RIGHT. JONES IS NEXT TO HIM, WALKER NEXT TO JONES.

WILSON	Platoon 'shun.

(FRAZER IS AHEAD OF THE SQUAD. THE SQUAD IS MORE OR LESS TOGETHER. JONES LAGS BEHIND, SO WE HAVE THREE MOVEMENTS.)

WILSON	Try and get it together. Stand at ease.

(SAME RESULT)

Squad 'shun.

(THE SAME RESULTS)

MAIN	Frazer, you're jumping the gun. Jones, you're lagging behind.

WILSON	Perhaps it would be best if I took them, after your lecture, and we'll try to negotiate some sort of compromise.
MAIN	Just get it right, Sergeant, that's all I ask. Now, men, I want you to squat in front of the platform for a lecture. Move.
FRAZER	(GALVANIZED INTO ACTION) Come on now, look lively there. Gather round the platform at the double.

(JONES GIVES THE SAME COMMAND A LITTLE LATER)

FRAZER	(SALUTES) Platoon present, sir, and ready for the lecture.
JONES	(SALUTING) Er... ready for lecture.
MAIN	Thank you, Corporals. (TURNS TO WILSON) Lots of keen NCOs here, Sergeant.
WILSON	Yes, haven't we just.
MAIN	Now, I want you to pay particular attention to what I'm about to say.
FRAZER	Pay attention there!
MAIN	The fact that Hitler hasn't kicked off with his invasion doesn't mean to say that the whistle's gone for 'no side'. It's quite on the cards he'll put recce parties ashore from submarines to find out the disposition of our forces.
FRAZER	That's right, you know. The Captain's right.
MAIN	Thank you, Frazer. Such parties could strike at any time, before church bells were rung – while we were still in our homes – and shops.
FRAZER	You might be in the bank, sir.
MAIN	Yes, quite right, Frazer. But we're going to be ready for them. Our watchword must be – 'they shall not pass'.
FRAZER	Beautiful words.
MAIN	So there we are, at home, probably without our guns, when suddenly a ruthless Nazi stormtrooper bursts through the door holding a Luger or a machine gun. There he stands, facing you. What are you going to do?
WALKER	I'll have done it.
FRAZER	That'll be enough of that. I've got his name, sir.
PIKE	Hear that, he's got your name.
WALKER	Yeah, I've got his whisky.
MAIN	Now, I daresay you think this situation is pretty hopeless.

(THE PLATOON NOD)

	Well, it's not – is it, Wilson?
WILSON	If you say not, sir.
MAIN	All you need is a clear head, steel nerve and a quick hand.
WALKER	And a tank.
FRAZER	That was Walker again, sir. I've got him, sir. Fall in two men.
WILSON	Frazer, don't let's be too hasty. Walker suggested that in the circumstances it would be

something of a comfort to have a tank as well as a cool head. I must say I rather agree with him.

MAIN   You don't need a tank in a situation like this, Wilson. You need guts. And know-how. You've all got the guts and by the time you leave this hall I'll have given you the know-how. Now, I want volunteers.

(FRAZER AND JONES LEAP FORWARD)

MAIN   Ah, two keen men, yes. You, Frazer, are a Nazi stormtrooper. Take this. (MAIN HANDS OVER HIS GUN) Now, Jones, I want you to imagine that you're in your shop this afternoon, going about your normal business. Got that?

JONES   Yes, sir.

MAIN   Right, now you, Frazer, enter the front door.

JONES   Permission to speak, sir.

MAIN   Yes, Jones.

JONES   I wasn't in my shop this afternoon, sir.

MAIN   Well, er ... we'll just imagine that you were.

JONES   Today's early, closing day you see, sir.

MAIN   Well, we'll ignore that for the time being. Frazer, you burst in – see Jones – and tell him to stick 'em up.

JONES   They say, sir. That's boch parlez-vous for stick 'em up.

MAIN   Thank you, Jones. Go on, Frazer.
Now, what are you going to do, Jones?

JONES   Put my handies hock, sir.

MAIN   Quite right. No sense in antagonizing

Lance Corporal Jones was a regular soldier with 29 years service. He signed on as a drummer boy in 1884 and took part in many campaigns, hence his chest full of medals which were carefully researched and are all genuine. Jones's most famous campaign was the Battle of Omdurman in 1898 under General Kitchener.

him. The next thing to do is fix him with a stare.

(JONES ADJUSTING HIS GLASSES, DOES SO)

MAIN   When you have his attention, you can distract him. Look at me, Frazer – look me in the eyes. Great Scott – look out!

(FRAZER LOOKS BEHIND HIM. MAINWARING WHIPS OUT A CHAIR AND LUNGES, JUST STOPPING SHORT OF FRAZER)

There, you see, it works.

WILSON   That was awfully good, sir.

FRAZER   It wasn't fair. I wasna ready.

MAIN   No, Frazer – and the bosch won't be ready either. Now I want you to take particular note of the way I used the chair. You must lunge with the legs – like that. (HE DEMONSTRATES)

GODFREY   Like a lion tamer, sir.

MAIN   Er, yes – yes, that's right, Godfrey. It's no good swiping at it like this – you must lunge. (HE DEMONSTRATES) So there you are, you can deal with a storm trooper with a gun.

JONES   There's just one thing, sir.

MAIN   Yes, Jones.

JONES   I don't have no chairs in my shop.

MAIN   Ah, don't you. Well I'm sure you could look round and improvise some other weapon.

WALKER   Perhaps you could make him sit on the bacon slicer, Jonesey.

MAIN   Don't be facetious, Walker. It's a very real enemy that we have to deal with.

FRAZER   Shall I take his name, sir?

MAIN   No thank you, Frazer.

WALKER   He's going to have a go!

GODFREY   Power corrupts, I'm afraid.

MAIN   Right, we'll deal with your problem later, Jones. In the meantime, another couple can have a try.

JONES   'Ere wait a minute, I 'aven't done the chair yet. I only fixed him with a stare.

MAIN   Oh, very well. One more volunteer.

FRAZER   Walker!

WALKER   I never said a word!

FRAZER   You're volunteering.

WALKER   Oh, am I?

MAIN   Oh, good man – up here, Walker, take the gun. Jones, you're going about your business.

JONES   I thought if you didn't mind, sir, that I'd be poking the fire.

MAIN   Yes, Jones, anything you like. Now, come in, Walker.

WALKER   Handy hoch!

JONES   Ah! (HE PUTS HIS HANDS UP) I'm fixing him with my stare. Ah, wass ist das?

WALKER   Eh?

JONES   That's German for 'what's that?'

WALKER   What's what?

MAIN   Your supposed to look round, Walker.

WALKER   Oh, sorry, sir. Do it again, Jonesey.

JONES   Was ist dass?

(WALKER LOOKS ROUND. WITH A YELL JONES DIVES FOR A CHAIR. IT IS THE END OF SIX AUDIENCE CHAIRS TOGETHER)

Jessie Mattthews was a famous dancer and musical comedy star of the 1920s and 30s.
Much later she became Mrs Dale in the BBC radio soap opera Mrs Dale's Diary.

Hang on.

(HE TRIES AGAIN AND YELLS)

WALKER   I reckon you're dead, Jonesey.

MAIN   Well, I think that has served to illustrate a very vital point. You must have your plan worked out.

JONES   Well, it's like I said, sir, I wouldn't have a chair in the shop.

MAIN   I was coming to that, Jones. If no weapon is at hand, you're probably thinking the situation is hopelss, but it's jolly well not. Here's what you do. You distract Jerry – just the same as before – and kick the gun from his hands – so. (HE GIVES A KICK AND STAGGERS. WILSON CATCHES HIM) It's all right, Wilson. Now – that's all very well for youngsters but some of us will need a bit of practice in order to kick high enough. Let's see you try – come along now.

(THEY ALL START TO REHEARSE HIGH KICK)

Up, up, up.

(HE CONTINUES TO ENCOURAGE THEM)

MAIN   Up – up – up. Come along, Wilson, you can do better than that.

WILSON   I'm sorry, sir, I was never much of a Jessie Matthews. (HE DOES TWO MORE KICKS) It's about time some of your tiller girls went on guard, sir.

MAIN   By jove, so it is! Fall in your guard, Frazer.

FRAZER   Fall in – the guard. Over here at the double. (WALKER, PIKE & GODFREY FALL IN) Smarten up your ideas there. Chin in, chest out, stomach in. Squad 'shun. Right turn. Guard ... to the command post, qui ... ck march. Right wheel double. (THEY DOUBLE) Right wheel. (HE DOUBLES THEM TWICE ROUND THE HALL. GODFREY STOPS AFTER THE FIRST CURCUIT AND CATCHES UP THE LAST TIME. THEY GO OUT OF THE DOOR GIVING EYES RIGHT ON THE WAY)

MAIN   (TO WILSON) I think I've picked the right one there, Wilson.

WILSON   Yes, sir. You've picked a right one!

FADE.

SCENE 4.
SIDE OFFICE.

FADE UP ON SIDE ROOM OF CHURCH HALL. A DUST SHEET COVERS THE DESK. A
PLANK BETWEEN TWO TRESTLES STAND AGAINST THE BOOK CASE OVER THE DESK
CHAIR. ENTER MAINWARING. HE LOOKS ROUND.

MAIN	Wilson! Wilson! (WILSON ENTERS FROM THE MAIN HALL)
WILSON	Yes, sir?
MAIN	What the devil's going on here?
WILSON	I gather the vicar found a couple of tins of whitewash and he and the verger decided to lighten their darkness.
MAIN	He might have had the courtesy to mention it. If Hitler had invaded unexpectedly last night, all this would have been damned awkward.

(HE MOVES ROUND IN FRONT OF THE CHAIR AND GRABS THE DUST SHEET)

MAIN	Give me a hand to get this off.
WILSON	Do you think we should? I mean, it is his desk.
MAIN	We'll have to get this situation clarified. I mean all that confusion over the ammunition and the altar candles would have looked very bad if the balloon had gone up.

(HE SITS)

Shove it away for now. We'll put it back after the parade.

(THERE IS A KNOCK AT THE DOOR)

Come in.

(ENTER FRAZER. HE SALUTES)

MAIN	Ah, Corporal Frazer. (HE RISES TO SALUTE AND KNOCKS HIS HEAD ON THE PLANK) This'll have to go, Wilson. All go well with the guard last night?
FRAZER	Aye, sir, it did. Here are the charge sheets.
MAIN	Charge sheets?
FRAZER	Aye, that's what I said. Charge sheets.

(MAINWARING PICKS THEM UP AND READS THEM)

MAIN	Private Pike deserting his post. Private Godfrey, cowardice in the face of the enemy. Private Walker, mutiny. These are rather serious charges, you know, Frazer.
FRAZER	I ken that fine, sir. And I hope you'll make an example of these men, sir, by dealing with them with the utmost severity.
MAIN	I see. Would you mind leaving a moment, Frazer. I'd like to talk to Sergeant Wilson about this.
FRAZER	Certainly, sir. I'll have the prisoners and escorts standing by.

(HE SALUTES. MAINWARING STANDS TO SALUTE AND BANGS HIS HEAD AGAIN)

WILSON	Shall I get some of the men to take these down, sir?
MAIN	Never mind that now. What are we going to do about these?
WILSON	I don't think we're allowed to put them on a charge.
MAIN	Neither do I. What punishment can we give? I can't give Pike C.B. We're shorthanded at the bank as it is.
WILSON	We can hardly dock their pay. They don't get any.
MAIN	What's even worse – all these charges on active service are court martial offenses

	carrying the death penalty!

WILSON   Perhaps you could give them a good talking-to.

MAIN   It's damned awkward.

WILSON   D'you think we could get Frazer to drop the charges?

MAIN   Not a chance.

WILSON   Perhaps we could drop Frazer.

MAIN   Come, come, Wilson. We must support our NCOs. (THERE IS A KNOCK AT THE DOOR) Come in!

(ENTER JONES. HE SALUTES – MAINWARING STANDS BUT REMEMBERS THE PLANK)

MAIN   Yes, Jones.

JONES   Captain Mainwaring, sir. I got a serious complaint. Lance Corporal Frazer just put me on a fizzer!

> **To be 'put on a fizzer' was an expression meaning to be put on a charge.**

(FRAZER, ENTERING BEHIND HIM)

FRAZER   Aye, there it is – it's on the sheet, you've got to go through with it.

JONES   He can't do this to me – I'm senior to him.

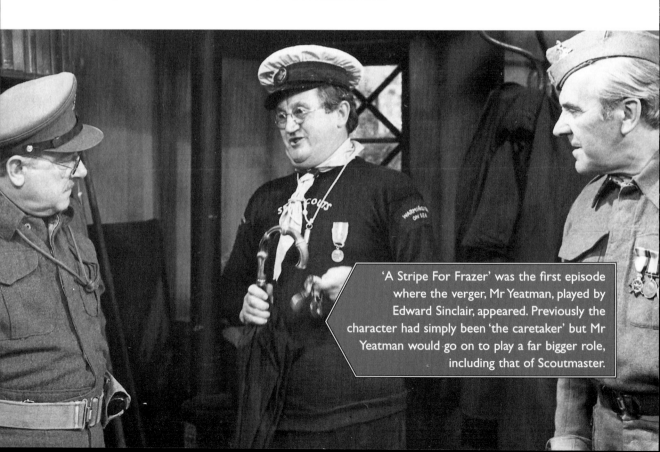

'A Stripe For Frazer' was the first episode where the verger, Mr Yeatman, played by Edward Sinclair, appeared. Previously the character had simply been 'the caretaker' but Mr Yeatman would go on to play a far bigger role, including that of Scoutmaster.

FRAZER   He called me a stupid old – what it says on that paper – in front of the men. That's conduct to the prejudice of good order.

MAIN   Now really, this has gone far enough. Get those other men in, Frazer.

FRAZER   Yes, sir. Prisoners – caps off. First prisoner and escort, quick march. Left right, left right, left right, left wheel ... halt! Right turn.

(PIKE, FLANKED BY TWO PRIVATES, ENTERS)

FRAZER   Second prisoner and escort quick march, left right, left right – le...ft wheel – right – halt, right turn. Prisoners reporting for trial, sir.

(HE SALUTES. MAINWARING RETURNS HIS SALUTE AND HITS HIS HEAD)

MAIN   This is ludicrous. Get all these escorts out of here. These aren't desperate criminals on the run, get 'em out.

FRAZER   Escorts, disss-miss.

(THE ESCORTS PUSH THROUGH THE CONFUSION TO GET BACK INTO THE HALL)

MAIN   And now get this damned plank out of the way.

JONES   I'll help you, Mr Mainwaring, sir.

(THEY REMOVE THE PLANK)

MAIN   Now, first things first. Now, what happened last night?

PIKE   Well, sir – I was in the slit-trench when a great big Alsation come up and barked at me and he wouldn't go away, so I went to the guard house to get help.

FRAZER   Deserting his post.

GODFREY   Well, Corporal Frazer told me to go and help Pike and I told him I didn't want to. You see, dogs don't like me, even quite little dogs. I seem to bring out the worst in them so I wouldn't go.

FRAZER   Cowardice in the face of the enemy.

MAIN   You can hardly call an Alsation an enemy.

FRAZER   The Nazis are facing us just across the water, sir.

MAIN   I see. Well - Walker?

WALKER   Well, I told Taffy here, if he went on being so regimental we'd stop his whisky.

FRAZER   Note that, sir – 'we'd stop his whisky', they'd conspired together – that's mutiny! and then just now, Corporal Jones – in front of my men - calling me a stupid old 'what's written on that piece of paper'.

JONES   Oh no I didn't. You said – I suppose you think I'm a stupid old 'what's on that paper'. I said yes.

(THE NEXT THREE SPEECHES ARE SPOKEN TOGETHER)

WALKER   How can it be mutiny to stop him getting whisky?

PIKE   I didn't desert. I just went to get help from the guard room.

GODFREY   I don't think it's very fair to go through this rigmarole just because dogs don't like me.

(THE VERGER HAS BEEN OVERHEARING THE LAST THIRTY SECONDS)

VERGER   Can I be getting on with the ceiling? I won't disturb you more than necessary.

MAIN   Really, this is the last straw! Can't you wait ten minutes, blast you!

    I'm going to have to sort this out with the vicar. If you ask me you're the silly old – what's on the paper.

(HE GOES)

MAIN   Now look here - I've had enough of this. I'm going to adjourn this case until I've had time to take legal advice. In the meantime, you'll all return to duties which are to prepare yourselves to defend your homes from Nazi assault. Is that understood?

FRAZER   Yes, sir! Prisoners – about–

JONES   Here – I'll do that. I'm the senior one.

MAIN   Get out! All of you! Get out.

FRAZER
& JONES   Yes, sir.

(THEY ALL GO)

MAIN   Wilson – I'm a patient man but I think I'm reaching the end of my tether.

WILSON   Yes, isn't it exasperating.

MAIN   I'd never have believed Frazer would have stirred up all this trouble.

WILSON   I did say I wasn't too keen.

MAIN   I know you did.

WILSON   As ye sow – so shall ye reap!

MAIN   I don't want any biblical quotations, Wilson. How to deal with it is the question?

(ENTER COLONEL SQUARE)

SQUARE   Mainwaring. (HE PRONOUNCES IT AS SPELT)

MAIN   Yes.

SQUARE   You remember me, Square. Square's the name.

MAIN   Oh yes, you were with Lawrence of Arabia, Colonel Square.

SQUARE   Corporal Colonel Square.

MAIN   Corporal, Colonel?

SQUARE   Of course it couldn't be Colonel Corporal could it? I've been attached to you by H.Q. to train you in guerrilla warfare.

MAIN   Oh, I see. Good.

SQUARE   It's good to be back in the saddle again, eh?

MAIN   We're not going through all that business with the horses again, are we?

SQUARE   Lord, no! Got to get those old-fashioned notions out of your head.

'Section 40' was a section of the Army Act which covered 'conduct to the prejudice of good order and military discipline.' Army form 252 was the number of the charge sheet.

(HE SEES THE CHARGE PAPERS ON THE TABLE)

> Good heavens! Two five two's – charge sheets. That takes me back. I haven't seen one of those since 1919. Got through five thousand of them in one month.

MAIN   Five thousand charge sheets!

SQUARE   Well, we were right out in the desert. We couldn't get anything else. What fool made these out?

WILSON   Why? Aren't they any good?

SQUARE   Mutiny isn't section forty, neither is cowardice. Hah, playing at soldiers. You're all the same, you chaps. Sir, are your men on parade?

WILSON   Yes, they're in the hall.

SQUARE   Right, I'll start licking them into shape.

(HE CROSSES TO DOOR)

> By the look of those charges, you need a bit of discipline around here.

(HE EXITS. OUT OF VISION WE HEAR HIS VOICE)

Right, fall in three ranks etc. etc.

MAIN   The whole thing is getting out of hand, Wilson. I shall be glad when today's over.

WILSON   But if these charges aren't properly made out you can drop them and that's the end of it.

MAIN   Yes, as long as we can stop our NCOs from making any more.

WILSON   Oh, I don't think you need worry about old Jones.

MAIN   We'd better talk to Frazer now – before anything else happens.

WILSON   I'll get him in.

(FRAZER STORMS IN)

FRAZER   You've done this deliberately!

(CROSSES TO THE STREET)

MAIN   Frazer! What's the matter now?

FRAZER   Yon maniac's put me on a bloody frizzer! (HE GOES)

MAIN   Frazer! – Wilson – get Square in here.

(SQUARE'S VOICE – OUT OF VISION- 'PRISONERS AND ESCORT – QUICK MARCH'.
GODFREY, PIKE AND WALKER ARE MARCHED IN, JONES IS AN ESCORT, WITH HIS
HAT ON. PRISONERS HAVE THEIR HATS OFF)

SQUARE   Left wheel, halt. Right turn.

MAIN   What in heaven's name is happening?

SQUARE   Slackest rabble I've ever seen. They're all on two five two. Idle on parade, sir. And I'm charging that NCO of yours with insolence!

JONES   (ENJOYING IT) Permission to speak, sir?

MAIN   Yes, Jones.

JONES   It was much worse than what was on that paper.

MAIN   Oh, really, this has got to stop. Wilson, get Frazer.

WILSON   (AT THE DOOR) He's gone, sir.

JONES   Deserting his post!

MAIN   I want him back here on the double. We've all got to come to an understanding. I can't have all my time taken up with these petty, fogging little charges.

WALKER   I don't think Frazer will be long, sir. He's only gone round the corner.

MAIN   What in heaven's name for?

WALKER   He's gone for a boat hook.

(CUT TO HALL – FRAZER ENTERS BRANDISHING A BOAT HOOK)

FRAZER   Where is he? Let me get at him?

(HE CHARGES TOWARDS THE OFFICE DOOR)

MAIN   Wilson – lock that door! Don't let him in.

(WE FADE ON FRAZER AS HE STARTS TO ATTACK THE DOOR WITH THE BOAT HOOK)

DAD'S ARMY NO. 12

Under Fire

CAST

Capt. George Mainwaring ....Arthur Lowe

Sgt. Arthur Wilson ....John Le Mesurier

L/Cpl. Jack Jones ....Clive Dunn

Pte. James Frazer ....John Laurie

Pte. Joe Walker ....James Beck

Pte. Charles Godfrey................................Arnold Ridley

Pte. Frank Pike ....Ian Lavender

Mrs Pike...Janet Davis

Corporal-Colonel Square.....................Geoffrey Lumsden

Capt. Bailey...John Ringham

Mrs Keen ....Queenie Watts

Mrs Witt ....Gladys Dawson

Sigmund Murphy ....Ernst Ulman

A.R.P. Warden ....Bill Pertwee

Woman ....June Petersen

Pte. Sponge ....Colin Bean

Remainder of Platoon...........................Richard Jacques
Frank Godfrey
Alec Coleman
Hugh Cecil
Jimmy Mac
Desmond Callum-Jones
Vic Taylor
David Seaforth
Richard Kitteridge

Never, Never Sell Your Rights

This was the last episode to be recorded in black and white. Within a short time, all the BBC studios were equipped to record in colour. The next series of *Dad's Army* in 1969 was in glorious colour and the show took off like a rocket. The whole country went crazy about us and within two years we were featured in a special Royal Command Show at the Television Theatre in Shepherds Bush.

When you work with a bunch of people over nine years, as David and I did with the *Dad's Army* team, you get to know them really well. The three members of the cast I gravitated towards were Bill Pertwee, Arnold Ridley and Arthur Lowe. There was no particular reason, it just happened. Bill had a great sense of humour, kept the atmosphere relaxed and was always fun to be with. Arnold and I used to talk for hours about writing. He had, in fact, written over thirty plays, including the great comedy classic, *The Ghost Train*. He said to me one day, 'You know, James, actors have no respect for the written word. Many years ago, I took a famous actor out to lunch. He was starring in one of my plays and all through the meal he told me what was wrong with it: too many characters, the first half ending was weak, and his part needed building up. We came out of the restaurant and walked down the street, with the actor still telling me how my play could be improved. We passed a stationer's shop, I told him to wait, went inside and came out with a notepad and pencils. I gave them to him and said, "Why don't you try writing your own play?"'

During the 1930s, Arnold formed a film company and it was very successful. The first film he produced did very well, then during the making of the second film, the bank behind him went bust and Arnold was left holding the baby. Rather than go bankrupt, he paid everyone off personally. To help raise the money, he sold the amateur rights to *The Ghost Train*. This play is ideally suited to amateur companies and scarcely a week goes by without the classic thriller being played in a church hall or similar venue in some corner of the globe. Over sixty-odd years it would have earned Arnold a fortune. He said to me, 'James, sell anything – even your mother-in-law – but never, never, sell your rights.'

Arthur Lowe and I had a very unusual thing in common – his father had been a butler and my grandfather had also been a butler, and we swapped stories that had been handed down in our respective families about domestic service at the turn of the century.

We also swapped stories about the years we had spent doing weekly rep. When he came out of the army after the war, Arthur's wife, Joan, got him a job with her in Harry Hanson's repertory company. So many Arthur Lowe stories have been recounted over the years, but I would like to finish with one that I am quite sure has never been told before. When we were out filming, I used to drive Arthur to location. One day, he said to me, 'You know that makeup girl, the voluptuous one with the curly hair?' 'Yes, Arthur,' I replied. There was a long pause and I couldn't believe it when I heard him say, 'I suppose they are all poking her, are they?' 'I have really no idea, Arthur,' I gasped. There was another long pause, we stopped at some traffic lights and he turned to me with a wistful look on his face and said, 'Of course, Joan would never tolerate anything like that, you know.'

Jimmy Perry

SCENES

1.   SIDE OFFICE. DAY
2.   ROOF OF CHURCH TOWER. NIGHT
3.   SIDE OFFICE. NIGHT
4.   EXT. OF HOUSE. NIGHT
5.   HALLWAY OF ABOVE. NIGHT
6.   SIDE OFFICE. NIGHT
7.   CHURCH HALL. NIGHT
8.   STAGE OF CHURCH HALL. NIGHT

SCENE 1.

SIDE OFFICE. DAY.

ENTER MAINWARING IN HIS TWEED SUIT WITH THE SUNDAY PAPERS. HE HANGS UP HIS TIN HAT AND HIS GAS MASK. HE TAKES OFF HIS MUFFLER AND HIS JACKET. WE SEE HE IS IN PYJAMAS. HE TAKES HIS UNIFORM OUT OF A CARRIER BAG AND PUTS IT ON THE DESK. HE REMOVES HIS TROUSERS REVEALING PYJAMA TROUSERS.

(ENTER WILSON)

WILSON   Good Lord! Er, did you sleep here, sir?

(MAINWARING IS PUTTING THE BUTTONS IN HIS UNIFORM JACKET)

MAIN   No, no. And more's the pity with those damned Jerry aircraft passing over all the time. I spent the night in the cupboard under the stairs. Elizabeth, you know, very nervous type. As soon as the siren goes, she's under the stairs. Wild horses wouldn't drag her out until the all clear. Scared out of her wits. I don't like leaving her on her own, so I have to go too.

WILSON   (HAVING HUNG UP HIS GAS MASK AND HELMET) Let me help, sir.
(HE HELPS WITH THE BUTTONS)

MAIN   To make matters worse, we have Elizabeth's mother staying with us. She sat on my chair all night with her gas mask open on her lap, clutching her pension book. I was on a camp stool with my elbow on the gas meter, my head resting on a coat hook.

WILSON   Dear, oh, dear. I spent the night under the kitchen table.(HE STARTS TO UNDRESS. HE IS ALSO IN HIS PYJAMAS)

MAIN   I didn't think you had a kitchen table.

WILSON   Oh, I was at a friend's house. There was so much shrapnel coming down from the ack ack guns that they wouldn't let me go home.

MAIN   Huh, lucky they had pyjamas to fit you, wasn't it?

WILSON   Yes, wasn't it?

(ENTER MRS PIKE)

MRS PIKE   Good morning, Mr Mainwaring.

(SHE HANDS WILSON HIS SHIRT AND TIE)

You'd forget your head if it wasn't screwed on.

WILSON   (WHISPERING) Mavis! I didn't need it and you were asleep.

MRS PIKE   Afraid I might wake up, were you? (EXIT)

MAIN   Hm. I had to leave mine as well. It was in the airing cupboard – in the bathroom. Elizabeth's mother was in residence. Extraordinary woman – she sits there for hours.

(ENTER COLONEL SQUARE, HE SALUTES)

MAIN   Ah, good morning, Corporal Square.

SQUARE   Corporal Colonel Square.

MAIN   Of course, Corporal Colonel Square. We weren't expecting you quite so soon.

SQUARE   So it seems. Came to prepare the morning's exercise.

(HE CROSSES TO THE DOOR, TURNS AND LOOKS AGAIN)

Extraordinary!

(HE GOES OUT)

MAIN   I think we had better get dressed as quickly as possible, before the rest of the platoon start trooping in.

WILSON   I quite agree, sir.

(MAINWARING TAKES OFF HIS PYJAMA TROUSERS TO REVEAL LONG JOHNS. WILSON IS TAKING OFF HIS PYJAMA TOP)

There was a real danger of casualties from 'friendly fire'. One of the first people to be killed in this way, strangely enough, was the famous music hall comedian, Harry Tate, in Dundee in February 1940.

| MAIN | I recommend that you get a pair of these before the winter sets in, Wilson. |
| WILSON | Funnily enough, I bought a pair last week, sir. |

(TAKES HIS TROUSERS OFF REVEALING A SIMILAR PAIR)

	I got them specially for when we are on guard. These denims aren't very thick.
MAIN	Yes. It gets damned draughty round by the waterworks. I'll be glad when the Eastgate platoon takes over.
WILSON	(ADMIRING MAINWARING'S LONG JOHNS) I must say, those look awfully cozy.
MAIN	(TURNING TO SHOW THEM OFF) Twenty-two and six – Mrs Nolan's. The little draper on the corner. Under the counter, of course. She has any amount of stuff hidden away, you know.
WILSON	So it seems. It must be quite an Aladdin's Cave.

(ENTER BAILEY)

| BAILEY | Good grief! |

(HE SALUTES)

	Good morning.
MAIN	Ah, good morning.
BAILEY	(NOT KNOWING WHAT TO SAY) Ah!
MAIN	Ah!
BAILEY	Well, er, shall I come back later?
MAIN	No, no. We're just changing into our uniforms.
BAILEY	Ah!
WILSON	Can we help you at all?
BAILEY	Ah, well the docks took a bit of a pasting down the coast last night.

‘Stop me and buy one’ was the slogan for Wall’s Ice Cream. The salesman would ride on a tricycle fitted with a freezer. He would ring the bell and shout, ‘Wall’s are lovely,’ or a similar cry. As the war went on, the ‘stop me and buy one’ man disappeared due to the shortage of supplies and the fact that the men were drafted into the forces.

MAIN	Did they, indeed? Poor devils. We heard them going over all night.
BAILEY	Well, of course, it may be your turn next. They are using enormous numbers of these incendiary bombs. The old man wants all units to put maximum strength on duty to help tackle them.
MAIN	You can count on my men to give every support.
BAILEY	Check on your sand and your water supplies. That’s the main thing.
MAIN	Make sure that’s done, Wilson.
BAILEY	How’s Square getting on with the guerrilla training?
MAIN	Huh, a bit old fashioned if you ask me.
BAILEY	He seemed full of ideas for harassing the enemy.
WILSON	You must admit, sir, he’s come up with one or two wheezes. The stop-me-and-buy-one, for instance.
MAIN	Filling choc ices full of Harpic? Hardly appropriate for modern warfare, Wilson.
SQUARE	(OFF) Foot soldier, right – point. Foot soldier, left – point. Etc.
MAIN	We’d better go and see what’s going on.

(THEY ENTER THE HALL. AS THEY OPEN THE DOOR SQUARE YELLS)

SQUARE Charge!

(PIKE, WALKER AND JONES ARE MOUNTED ON BICYCLES. THEY PEDDLE ACROSS TOWARDS MAINWARING & CO. YELLING AS THEY GO. MAINWARING, WILSON AND BAILEY DODGE ASIDE. JONES GOES STRAIGHT THROUGH THE DOORWAY AND CRASHES INTO THE DESK)

MAIN Great Scott! What's going on? What are you doing, Square?

SQUARE Just getting them up in the saddle, Mainwaring, getting them mobile.

MAIN But you'll smash every bicycle in the place.

SQUARE Well, there's no shortage of bikes, is there?

MAIN No, but there's a shortage of meat – and that butcher is valuable. What a disaster.

WILSON Are you all right, Jonesey?

JONES Sorry, Mr Mainwaring, sir. I had me sabre in me brake hand. I've broken me pump.

MAIN Lucky you didn't do yourself an injury, Jones.

JONES I'd have done the Jerries an injury. They'd have had my cold steel right up 'em, sir. They wouldn't have liked it, sir.

SQUARE No good at all. You're not on a Sunday School ride. You're killing Nazis.

WALKER Would it be more frightening if we rang our bells?

(HE DOES SO. ENTER JONES)

SQUARE Back to your place, Walker.

MAIN What's going on, Corporal?

SQUARE Forming a mobile striking force, sir. Swift and silent, sabre slashing – thrusting where the enemy least expects it – on bicycles. (TO MEN) Now, let's have another go.

MAIN That'll be enough of that for the time being. I want to address the men.

JONES I'm afraid I can't do any more charging until I get a new pump.

MAIN Fall them in, Corporal.

SQUARE Corporal Colonel Square.

WILSON Fall in three ranks, you chaps.

MAIN Thank you, Sergeant. Hurry up, Walker.

WALKER (STILL HOLDING THE BIKE) Well, what am I supposed to do with this?

MAIN Don't argue. Fall in.

(WALKER THROWS THE BIKE DOWN.
MAINWARING LEAPS BACK TO AVOID IT)

MAIN Ha, that's more like it. Settle down, there. Squad, squa-a-d -

SQUARE Wrong.

MAIN (TAKING NO NOTICE) Squad, squa-a-ad -

SQUARE Wrong.

Wilson is always coming out with little bits of information about his service in World War I, including the fact that he was an officer and has medals. This particularly upsets Mainwaring, who has nothing. We used this theme in several later episodes to great effect.

MAIN   I beg your pardon?

SQUARE You're giving the wrong command, Mainwaring. We aren't a squad, we're a platoon.

MAIN   I'm sure what you say is correct, but these chaps here are fighting troops, not parade ground wallahs. Results are what we're after not a load of bull. Squad – er – platooooon, atten-shun.

(THEY COME TO A RAGGED ATTENTION)

MAIN   That was a very sloppy movement, Jones.

SQUARE It was a sloppy command. You want to put some snap into it, man. Platoon, stand at ease.

(THEY DO IT TOGETHER)

Platoon, atten-shun!

(THE SAME AGAIN)

SQUARE There you are, you see? When they hear a proper word of command, they jump to it.

MAIN   I am sure we are all very grateful to you for your help, Corporal Square.

SQUARE Corporal Colonel Square.

WILSON (HAVING EDGED CLOSE TO SQUARE SUDDENLY HE IS PROMPTED FOR THE FIRST AND PROBABLY THE LAST TIME IN HIS LIFE TO BEHAVE LIKE A SERGEANT. HE BARKS) Silence in the ranks!

(SQUARE LOOKS ROUND IN SURPRISE)

Look to your front. Did you shave this morning?

(SQUARE, COMPLETELY SURPRISED LOOKS
ROUND TOWARDS WILSON AGAIN)

WILSON   Look to your front. Next time, stand nearer the razor.

(IN DEAD SILENCE WILSON GOES TO
MAINWARING AND SALUTES)

WILSON   Platoon ready for your inspection, sir.

MAIN   (RETURNING HIS SALUTE, SAYS ALMOST UNDER HIS BREATH) Well done, Wilson.

WILSON   That's nothing, sir. A little bit I picked up at Catterick.

MAIN   Now, pay attention, please. So far, Hitler has lacked the courage to come and scrap with us toe to toe. Instead he is using a new and cowardly weapon; aerial attack with the fire bomb. Now, you all know how to deal with those but we must check that our equipment is in tip-top condition. Frazer, you've been responsible for the stirrup pump, is it in working order?

FRAZER   Yes, sir. I'll bring it round after parade.

MAIN   Bring it round? Why isn't it here?

FRAZER   I was using it for the dig for Victory Campaign in my garden. My apples had the blight.

MAIN   This is a vital piece of military equipment. It must not leave our headquarters. I take it you didn't borrow the water as well?

FRAZER   No, sir. Only the bucket.

MAIN   See they are returned, Wilson. And, Jonesy, check the sand buckets and the extinguisher. Oh, and the long handled shovel.

Not only the Home Guard, but also most of the civilian population were trained in how to deal with incendiary bombs and did their share of duty as fire watchers.

> Corporal Colonel Square had appeared in a couple of previous episodes. In the early days of the formation of the Home Guard, veterans of World War I flocked to join. As many of them were former high-ranking officers and could not keep their original ranks, a compromise was reached, hence the two titles Corporal Colonel. Their present rank came first. The character disappeared and came back in episode 28. We had promoted him to captain and put him in charge of the Eastgate platoon. He became Captain Mainwaring's arch rival. Geoffrey Lumsden was perfectly cast as Captain Square.

(JONES WHISPERS TO WALKER)

MAIN	Don't tell me that's been borrowed.
JONES	Yes, sir. For the command post stove, sir.
MAIN	I'm sure you don't need a twelve-foot shovel for the command post stove.
WALKER	You do for nicking the coal from the railway siding.
MAIN	(TURNING TO SERGEANT) Wilson.
WILSON	I'll see they're brought back, sir.
MAIN	(TO BAILEY) Ha, well, you can rest assured that this unit will be one hundred percent prepared by the time the sirens blow. Spotters will be posted on the church tower. The rest of us will be a mobile fire-fighting force.
BAILEY	Well, I hope you won't get any action. If you do, good luck.

SCENE 2.
THE ROOF OF CHURCH TOWER.

FRAZER AND GODFREY ARE ON GUARD, TIN-HATTED. IT IS NIGHT. THERE IS A HEAVY DRONE FROM THE AIRCRAFT OVERHEAD. SEARCHLIGHTS PROBE THE SKY.

FRAZER	My, there's a lot come over tonight.
GODFREY	There must be hundreds.
FRAZER	You're trembling like a leaf. Are you cold?
GODFREY	No, just frightened.
FRAZER	(LOOKING UP) Aye, I'm not blaming you.
GODFREY	It's not them so much, it's being up so high. I've always been the same. When I was in the Civil Service Stores I could have had a marvellous job in Accounts, but it was on the fifth floor. How much longer before we get relieved?
FRAZER	Twenty minutes.
GODFREY	I'll just pop down for a minute.
FRAZER	Man, you've been down there three times already. Why don't you go over there by the gargoyle?

GODFREY   Wouldn't that be sacrilege?

FRAZER   What would you do if a parachutist started coming down?

GODFREY   I don't know. War doesn't suit me I'm afraid. It's not that I'm a conscientious objector or anything like that, I'm just not very good at it.

FRAZER   (SEEING SOMETHING) What's that over there?

GODFREY   Where?

FRAZER   That light.

GODFREY   Oh, it's going on and off.

FRAZER   Damn it, man, I believe they're signalling.

GODFREY   Who would do a thing like that?

FRAZER   Where is it?

GODFREY   It's on the corner of Mortimer Street, near where the bomb dropped last night.

FRAZER   We'll go and tell the Captain.

SCENE 3.
SIDE OFFICE.

CUT TO MR MAINWARING IN THE SIDE OFFICE.

MAIN   Are you sure you're not mistaken, Frazer?

FRAZER   Absolutely. We both saw it.

MAIN   I'll phone the police.

SQUARE   Why waste time phoning them? You have the authority. You're on active service – act.

MAIN   I'll make the decisions here, Square. This is police

'Godfrey's not very nimble on his pins, I'm afraid.'

business, don't you think so, Wilson?

WILSON   I'm certain it isn't ours, sir.

SQUARE   Isn't it? What if it's a Jerry paratrooper marking the target?

FRAZER   Let's go and get him, sir.

MAIN   Very well. When action is needed, I'm the first to take it. You know where it is, Godfrey, lead the way.

GODFREY   Er, er, could you give me a moment or two before we go?

MAIN   Certainly not, every second is vital. You stay here, Square. Come with me, Wilson.

SCENE 4.
EXT. OF HOUSE.

CUT TO DOOR OF HOUSE. IT SHOULD BE THE THREE STOREY VICTORIAN TERRACE-TYPE HOUSE. BESIDE THE DOOR ARE THREE BELL BUTTONS, INDICATING THAT THE HOUSE IS DIVIDED INTO THREE FLATS. THERE IS A SMALL OVERHANGING PORCH OVERHEAD. SIMILAR HOUSES ARE SEEN IN THE BACKGROUND. HEAVY ACK ACK FIRE AND OVERHEAD BURSTS ARE HEARD. ENTER MAINWARING AND WILSON IN GREAT RUSH.

WILSON   Heavens, did you hear that shrapnel falling? A lump missed you by inches.

MAIN   I know, I heard it. Are Frazer and Godfrey all right?

WILSON   (LOOKING ROUND) Frazer's helping him. Godfrey's not very nimble on his pins, I'm afraid.

MAIN   Top floor, wasn't it?

(HE RINGS THE BELL. FRAZER AND GODFREY ARRIVE)

MAIN   Come under here, you two.

FRAZER   My, it's coming down.

MAIN   Are you sure this is the one, Frazer? (HE FEELS FOR A MATCH)

FRAZER   Aye, that's the one.

MAIN   Let's see what the name is. (HE STRIKES A MATCH)

VOICE OF
WARDEN   Put that light out, you bloody lunatic!

(MAINWARING QUICKLY PUTS THE MATCH OUT)

MAIN   Damn, I didn't see it.

WILSON   I did, sir. It was Murphy.

MAIN   Murphy? That's suspicious. This could be a nasty business.

GODFREY   Would you like my flashlight, sir? (HE HANDS IT OVER)

WILSON   Somebody's coming, sir. (THE DOOR OPENS. A SHORT FAT CONTINENTAL

> **In 'Branded', a later episode, it turns out that Godfrey had, in fact, been a conscientious objector, much to Mainwaring's horror. Later it emerges that Godfrey enrolled as a stretcher–bearer and had been decorated for bravery.**

GENTLEMAN IS REVEALED. HE HAS A THICK GERMAN ACCENT)

MURPHY	Please?
MAIN	Ah, are you Mr Murphy?
MURPHY	Vot is it you are vanting?
MAIN	One of my men saw a light flashing on and off at your flat.
MURPHY	Don't be so damned ridiculous. Who are you? (HE SHINES HIS TORCH IN MAINWARING'S FACE)
MAIN	I – I'm Captain Mainwaring, Home Guard. What's more to the point, who are you? (HE SHINES HIS TORCH IN MURPHY'S FACE)
MURPHY	My name is Murphy. Sigmund Murphy.
MAIN	You're not English, are you?
MURPHY	What are you talking about? I have lived here for twenty-five years.
FRAZER	You don't sound like an Englishman.
MURPHY	For that matter, my friend, neither do you.
WILSON	Where were you born, Mr Murphy?
MURPHY	I was born in Salzburg.
FRAZER	That's Germany, isn't it?
MURPHY	No, it is not. It is Austria, but I am a naturalised Englishman.
MAIN	Well, why do you call yourself Murphy?
MURPHY	With a war on, how would you like to be called Von Schickenhausen?
MAIN	Anyway, the point is, one of my men saw you flashing a light as if making a signal.
WOMAN'S VOICE	(AS IF FROM UPPER WINDOW) He was doin' it last night and all.
MURPHY	(SHOUTING) Why do you say such damned lies?
WOMAN	Oh, yes, you was. Just before the bomb dropped.
MURPHY	Are you mad? Do you think I signal so they drop a bomb on me?(TO MAINWARING) You don't want to take any notice of her. She is an interfering old cow. (SHOUTS) What about all those sailors that are visiting your flat, ha?
WOMAN	I'll have you for libel.
MURPHY	And the Canadian Airforce.
WILSON	Don't you think we ought to go inside before a scene develops?
MAIN	Yes, I think it might be advisable.

SCENE 5.
HALLWAY OF HOUSE.

THEY GO INSIDE INTO THE HALLWAY AND CLOSE THE DOOR.

MAIN	Now, Mr Murphy, what have you to say about this signalling?

MURPHY   I tell you, I was not doing the signalling.

FRAZER   You're German, though, aren't you?

MURPHY   I'm as British as you are.

(GODFREY WHISPERS TO MAINWARING)

MAIN   What is it, Godfrey?

(GODFREY WHISPERS AGAIN)

Oh, not now, for heaven's sake.

FRAZER   He's a German. I know damned well he's a German.

(MRS KEEN, MIDDLE-AGED BLONDE LADY COMES DOWNSTAIRS CARRYING A DACHSHUND)

MRS KEEN   Would you mind keeping your dog under control, he's been in my room again. (SHE HANDS HIM THE DACHSHUND)

FRAZER   There look, that's a German dog.

MURPHY   Fritz, come here, you bad boy.

FRAZER   He's even got a German name.

MRS KEEN   Damned foreigners. You ought to be interned.

MURPHY   Why don't you mind your own business?

(MRS WITT, A LITTLE OLD LADY EMERGES BEHIND THEM FROM THE CUPBOARD UNDER THE STAIRS)

MRS WITT   It's your moment of triumph, isn't it? Twenty-five years he's been plotting all this.

MURPHY   Get back in your cupboard, you old hag.

MRS WITT   He's a spy.

MURPHY   Don't be so ridiculous.

MRS KEEN   You ought to be done away with.

MAIN   Oh, come, come, madam.

MRS KEEN   He's in my room every night, eating my slippers.

MURPHY   I think she is talking about my dog.

(THE WOMAN OPPOSITE ENTERS)

WOMAN
OPPOSITE   He was signalling last night, no matter what he says. Nazi!

MURPHY   I am not a Nazi. I am British.

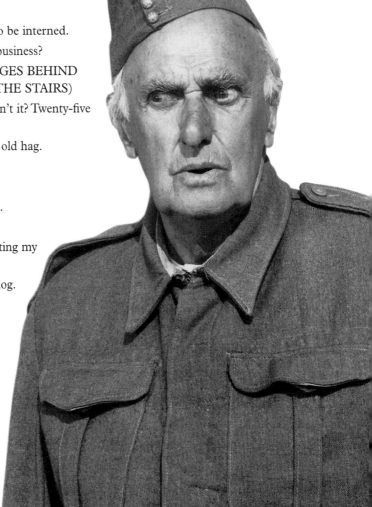

'He's a German. I know damned well he's a German.'

Corporal Colonel Square – note the Corporal's stripes and the Colonel's pips on his uniform.

MRS WITT   And there's a very often a strong smell of foreign garlic coming from his kitchen.

WOMAN
OPPOSITE   And he walks out of cinemas while they're still playing 'God Save the King'.

MAIN   Does he indeed? The evidence against you looks pretty strong, Mr Murphy. I'm taking you into custody so the police can investigate.

MURPHY   The world has gone mad.

WILSON   Do you think that's wise, sir?

MAIN   I take full responsibility, Wilson.

> At that time very few people in Britain cooked with Garlic. Anyone who did was regarded with suspicion. The stink of garlic or anything else foreign, like men who used eau–de–Cologne or wore suede shoes was completely beyond the pale.

GODFREY   (TO MURPHY) Before we go, do you think I could wash my hands?

MURPHY   Certainly not.

MAIN   By God, I think he is German. Bring him along.

SCENE 6.
SIDE OFFICE.

CUT TO SIDE OFFICE. SQUARE IS AT THE DESK ON THE PHONE.

SQUARE   Right, if there are any suspects, I'll hold them until we can hand 'em over to the civil power ... What are you worried about? I'm in command ... very funny ... right, well I'm coming back there as soon as I can hand over. You sound as if you need me ... I don't see what a hole in the head has to do with it.

(THE OTHER END HAS OBVIOUSLY HUNG UP. ENTER MRS PIKE FROM THE CHURCH HALL)

MRS PIKE   Frank forgot his balaclava. Where is he?

SQUARE   He's fire-spotting on the church tower.

MRS PIKE   He'll get his death. I'm going to have words about this. (SHE GOES OUT OF THE OUTSIDE DOOR. ENTER PIKE FROM THE CHURCH HALL)

PIKE   Here, Corp.

SQUARE   Corporal Colonel.

PIKE   Er, Corporal Colonel, it's getting a bit hot up there. There's lumps of shrapnel coming down like hail.

SQUARE   Get back to your post, boy.

PIKE   But if one of those pieces hits me, I'll be killed.

SQUARE   That's what soldiers are for. Get back.

(PIKE GOES OUT THROUGH THE OUTSIDE DOOR. THERE IS A RENEWED SOUND OF ACK ACK. SQUARE CROSSES TO PEEP THROUGH THE BLACKOUT)

SQUARE   That's right, let 'em have it.

(MAIN AND WILSON RUSH IN BREATHLESS)

WILSON   I didn't care for that very much.

MAIN   I quite agree, Wilson. Being brave is all very well, but it's damned frightening.

> **The police were always inundated with people saying their neighbours were fifth columnists and signalling to the enemy. Everyone thought the country was teeming with German spies, saboteurs and fifth columnists. In fact, there were very few German spies and those that did land were quickly caught. The so-called fifth columnists never existed, but at the height of the invasion scare, the Home Guard stopped and demanded proof of identity from everyone, even each other.**

(FRAZER ENTERS WITH GODFREY AND MURPHY)

MAIN   Bring him in here, Frazer.

SQUARE   Is this your prisoner?

MURPHY   You'll be the laughing stock, that's what you'll be. The laughing stock.

SQUARE   Sounds like a blasted Hun.

MURPHY   I tell you I'm a British Citizen.

SQUARE   I've told command. They're advising the civil power.

WILSON   The who?

SQUARE   The police, man. The police.

MAIN   The point is, what do we do with him in the meantime?

SQUARE   In the desert we used to tie them to the wheel of a gun carriage and leave them in the sun.

MAIN   That hardly meets the exigencies of the present emergency, Square.

SQUARE   Well, work something out, Mainwaring. You have to stand on your own feet sooner or later. I've been called back to H.Q.

MAIN   Have you? Then we'll try to manage without you.

SQUARE   I wish I'd had you in the desert, Mainwaring. I might have made a soldier out of you.

(HE CROSSES TO THE DOOR, TURNS AND LOOKS HIM UP AND DOWN)

Damn it, I don't believe even I could have done it. (HE GOES OUT)

MAIN   Damned arrogance. I'm going to see the General about him.

GOD   You won't be needing me for a minute or two, will you, sir?

(PIKE RUSHES IN)

PIKE   There's incendiaries coming down all over the place, sir.

(THERE'S A NOISE IN THE HALL, WALKER ENTERS)

WALKER   Blimey, there's one come in through the roof.

JONES   (ENTERING WITH THEM) It's all lit up sir. It's all lit up.

MAIN   Right, Wilson, you guard him. Frazer, give a hand outside. We'll deal with the one in the hall.

JONES   (RUNNING UP AND DOWN) Don't panic, anybody. Keep calm. Don't panic.

MAIN   Jones, get some water.

JONES   Yes, sir. I wasn't panicking, sir.

MAIN   Walker, you pump. Godfrey, you feed the hose through. I'll take the nozzle.

WILSON   Er, it's the jet for the fire and the spray for the bomb, sir.

MAIN   I know that, get out of the way.

(WALKER ARRANGES THE PUMP AND A BUCKET. GODFREY GETS DOWN ON HIS HANDS AND KNEES TO FEED THE HOSE THROUGH THE DOOR. MAINWARING GETS DOWN TO CRAWL THROUGH THE DOOR.)

MAIN   Where's the end?

GOD   I – I – I'm trying to find it, sir.

SCENE 7.
CHURCH HALL

JONES ENTERS THE MAIN HALL. HE CROSSES UNDER THE GALLERY. WHERE THE
FIRE BUCKET IS HUNG HEAD HIGH. HE UNHOOKS THE HANDLE FROM THE
BRACKET. THE BOTTOM OF THE BUCKET IS SUPPORTED BY ANOTHER METAL
BRACKET WHICH TIPS THE CONTENTS OF THE BUCKET RIGHT OVER HIM. HE
STAGGERS WITH THE BUCKET INTO THE OFFICE DOOR, MEETING MAINWARING
COMING OUT.

JONES   (SPURTING OUT A MOUTHFUL OF WATER) It's empty, sir.

MAIN   Well, fill it from the static water tank outside.

(JONES TURNS TO RUN TO THE DOOR. HE SLIPS AND FALLS WHILE DOING SO. HE FINALLY SCRAMBLES UP AND GOES OUT. MAINWARING GOES DOWN ON HIS HANDS AND KNEES TO APPROACH THE BOMB.)

(CALLING BEHIND HIM) Water on!

(WALKER STARTS TO PUMP. MAINWARING IS A LONG WAY FROM THE BOMB)

More hose, it's too far away.

(MAIN CRAWLS FORWARD. GODFREY, WALKER, THE BUCKET AND THE PUMP FOLLOW, STILL PUMPING)

I need more hose, damn you.

(MAIN TUGS HARD. IT COMES OFF THE PUMP)

That's more like it. Water on.

(WALKER PUMPS HARD. WATER SPURTS FROM THE SIDE NOZZLE OF THE PUMP LANDING ON GODFREY'S BACKSIDE)

GODFREY   Captain Mainwaring, sir, I wonder if I could possibly be excused for a moment or two?

MAIN   Certainly not. Walker, why don't you pump, blast you.

WALKER   I am doing, sir.

MAIN   Do it harder.

(WALKER PUMPS HARDER AND THEN SEES WHAT'S HAPPENING).

FRAZER   Blimey, it's come off.

MAIN   I don't believe it.

(HE RISES AND CROSSES. JONES RUNS IN CLUTCHING A SECOND BUCKET OF WATER TO HIS CHEST. HE SLIPS BACKWARD ON THE WET PART OF THE FLOOR, DRENCHING THE SECOND BUCKET OVER HIM. MAIN HELPS HIM UP)

MAIN   What are you doing, Jones?

JONES   (SPURTING OUT A MOUTHFUL OF WATER) Sorry, sir. (HE POURS A FEW DROPS INTO THE OTHER BUCKET) Every little helps. (HE GOES HALF AWAY AND THEN COMES BACK) My old dad used to say that, sir. (HE GOES FOR ANOTHER BUCKET. GODFREY IS TRYING TO PUT THE HOSE BACK ON THE PUMP)

MAIN   Hurry up and fix it, Godfrey.

GODFREY   I'm trying. Has anyone got a little screwdriver?

WALKER   (PRODUCING ONE) Here you are, three and a tanner.

PIKE   What about using the fire extinguisher on the stage, sir.

MAIN   Good idea, Pike.

(THEY CROSS THE HALL TO THE STAGE).

SCENE 8.
STAGE.

    MAIN   Right, grab it, Pike.

(PIKE TAKES DOWN THE CONE-SHAPED FIRE EXTINGUISHER FROM BEHIND THE PROSCENIUM. NOTE: THIS IS A NON-PRACTICAL ONE. THEY ARE BOTH NOW ON THE STAGE)

    Now, strike the knob.

(PIKE TURNS IT UPSIDE DOWN AND HITS IT WITH HIS HAND)

    Not like that. Strike it on the floor.

(PIKE RAISES IT)

    Not too hard.

(PIKE TAPS IT GENTLY)

    Well, harder than that.

(PIKE TAPS IT FRACTIONALLY HARDER)

    Oh, give it to me.

(MAIN RAISES THE EXTINGUISHER HIGH AND DRIVES IT DOWN ON THE FLOOR. IT GOES STRAIGHT THROUGH THE STAGE AND DISAPPEARS)

    VOICES   Hurry up, sir. It's catching on.

(MAIN PLUNGES HIS HAND INTO THE HOLE AFTER THE EXTINGUISHER)

    MAIN   Give me a hand, Pike.

    PIKE   Can you feel it, sir?

    MAIN   No, get out of the light.

(MAIN LOOKS INTO THE HOLE. A JET OF FOAM, AS IF FROM THE EXTINGUISHER, SHOOTS INTO HIS FACE. WILSON COMES UP TO MAINWARING)

    WILSON   Er, do you think you could hurry up, sir?

    MAIN   What do you think I'm trying to do?

    WILSON   It's just that I think it's spreading.

    MAIN   Well, get water and get back and guard Jerry.

(MRS PIKE JOINS THE GROUP)

MRS PIKE   Frank, I've been looking all over for you. Get this on. (SHE HAS A BALACLAVA WITH HER).

    MAIN   Not now, Mrs Pike.

MRS PIKE   He'll catch his death running around like this.

(JONES ENTERS WITH ANOTHER BUCKET. HE TRIUMPHANTLY SUCCEEDS IN PUTTING IT BESIDE THE FIRST. HE RUNS TO MAINWARING)

    JONES   Permission to speak, sir.

MAIN   What is it, Jones?

JONES   I brought another bucket of water, sir.

MAIN   (AS THE FOAM DIES DOWN) Good. I think we'd better try it.

(AS THEY CROSS ANOTHER MEMBER OF THE SQUAD GRABS THE BUCKET AND RUNS OUT VIA THE OFFICE)

JONES   Here, come back, that's my bucket.

MAIN   I know. The long-handled shovel, where is it?

WALKER   Outside the office, sir.

(THEY CROWD INTO THE OFFICE. FRAZER ENTERS WITH THE LONG-HANDLED SHOVEL. IT IS VERY LONG)

FRAZER   How about this, sir?

MAIN   Great minds think alike, Frazer. Now round here with it.

(THEY TRY TO GET THE SHOVEL INTO THE OFFICE AND ROUND THROUGH THE DOOR INTO THE HALL)

MAIN   Er, er, take it further out. Now try it higher up.

(THERE IS A LOT OF AD LIB TOING AND FROING. MURPHY TRIES TO HELP)

MAIN   Don't you touch it.

WALKER   Why don't we cut it in half?

(MRS PIKE ENTERS)

MAIN   Out of the way, woman. We are trying to deal with this fire bomb.

MRS PIKE   It's out.

MAIN   It's what?

MRS PIKE   It's out. I put a sand bag on it.

(ENTER THE IRATE WARDEN THROUGH THE OUTSIDE DOOR INTO THE OFFICE)

WARDEN   Now look here. I've had a serious complaint from the Head Warden that someone's been signalling to those planes overhead.

MAIN   Don't worry, warden. We have apprehended the alleged culprit. My men spotted him. He was in the house at the corner of Mortimer Street.

WARDEN   Oh, no. It's this door he's on about. It's been opening and shutting and showing a blinding light every time a fresh wave comes over. You've got a rotten apple in your barrel. Now, who is it? (HE LOOKS ROUND) Hullo, Siggy. What are you doing here?

MAIN   This is the man who has been signalling, and what's more, he's German.

WARDEN   Oh, no, he's not. He's a British subject and what's more, he was married to my Auntie Ethel.

MURPHY   They told the whole street I was a spy.

WARDEN   Oh no. This is where the spy is, mate. This is where the signal come from. You ask the Head Warden.

(PIKE RUSHES IN FROM THE HALL DOOR)

PIKE   There's another stick of fire bombs, sir. They've fallen right across the street.

MAIN   Right, out you go, fellas. Grab the pump, Walker. Bring the water, Jones, and all the sandbags you can lay your hands on.

(AS THEY CROSS THE HALL, THE FRONT ONE SLIPS ON THE WET PATCH AND THEY ALL COLLAPSE IN A HEAP. MURPHY AND WILSON ARE LEFT IN THE OFFICE)

MURPHY   You know, we Breetish are a vonderful people. We are brave, we have the great sense of humour, but I don't see how we are going to win the war.

WILSON   Yes, I must say that thought does occur to me from time to time.

(FADE ON THE MOB TRYING TO DISENTAGLE THEMSELVES).

Note that Hodges is wearing a dark helmet in this photo. This was before Hodges had been promoted to Chief Warden.

From the beginning of Season Three, *Dad's Army* was recorded in colour and the show became an enormous success. Eighty episodes were made, with the final one featuring Jonesey's wedding (he married Mrs Fox), ending the series with a celebration, a toast to the Home Guard and a message of hope for the future.